Contents

To Nancy,
the love of my life
—John

CHAPTER 1

Introduction

The topics of spirituality, intimacy, and sexuality necessarily commingle in our lives and in the lives of our counseling clients and spiritual directees. We sense God's invitation to acknowledge these three themes in interrelationship. Our effort has been worthwhile if what follows is helpful in some way to those of us who desire a healthy relationship between spirituality, intimacy, and sexuality.

We are encouraged in this effort by a story and a prayer. The story is found in John 12:1–7. There we find Martha's sister Mary anointing Christ, wiping his feet with her hair. It is related that one of the disciples, Judas Iscariot, rebuked her for using the expensive and fragrant oil in that manner when it could have been sold to aid the poor. Jesus, however, defended her—he understood and took into himself her great love for him.

What would it have been like to witness the reactions of those in the room? Perhaps some were embarrassed, stunned even, to witness Mary's communion with Jesus. What she did was at once spiritual, sensual, and intimate. She gave herself completely to Christ; he accepted her as only he could. As Christians we talk, study, sing, and pray about giving ourselves completely to God. But to see Mary actually do it must have evoked an array of responses from those present. Indeed, it still would today. She loved him with all of herself. She didn't bracket her sexuality, or put it aside, to be spiritually intimate with Jesus.

It is an astounding, lovely, and profound example of spirituality, intimacy, and sexuality as one.

The prayer that encourages us is found in John 17 within the context of the Last Supper discourses unique to that Gospel. It speaks of what Jesus most wants for us. He wants for us the kind of relationship with the Father that is his. He wants us to have that kind of relationship with each other. We know that this is a priority for Jesus because he repeats it in various ways throughout this Johannine prayer. He is saying that this is very, very important. He prays that we may be one as he and the Father are one. This prayer is God's invitation to intimacy—with him, with ourselves, and with each other. It is simultaneously an invitation to communion with God and to communion with others. You might say "What others?" The response is "All others." One is reminded of those extremely challenging words of nineteenth-century priest-poet Gerard Manley Hopkins, SJ:

> But thou bidst, and just thou art,
> Me shew mercy from my heart
> Towards *my brother, every other*
> *Man my mate and counterpart.*[1]

Intimacy is the practice of knowing another and allowing oneself to be known. God is calling us to know him completely and to allow ourselves to be completely known. He invites us to relate in that way to our sisters and brothers in Christ and ultimately to everyone. If you're not intimidated by the prospect of living this way, you have very different people in your life than we do. The people we know sometimes disappoint us. On occasion they betray our confidence. We risk being embarrassed or hurt by them. They are not entirely reliable. They have problems and challenges, for pity's sake! And those are just our fellow believers. By all this we mean to say that they are just like us:

poor prospects with which to practice this intimacy that God wants for us. We may desire this kind of intimacy in our minds, but it is not in our nature to practice it, indeed to risk it. Our natural instinct for self-preservation is much too strong to make ourselves that vulnerable without a guarantee that we won't be betrayed. It is likely, however, that someday there will be betrayal of some sort. It has probably already happened, as it did to Jesus, who nonetheless was intimate to the end.

It is Jesus' experience, in fact, that points to another facet of this intimacy to which God calls us. It is so profound, so God-given, that it is not contingent on the response it evokes. Jesus practiced intimacy with his Father, with those around him, and with persons who varied greatly in their ability to respond genuinely to him. The life of Jesus and his prayer tell us that intimacy is so vital to our well-being that its practice must not be conditional. Returning to Mary's anointing of Jesus, it was as if her act proclaimed: "This is between my Savior and me. You will have to contend with your own response to it." Hers was an unself-conscious and courageous intimacy, impervious to betrayal or even the praise of others.

For that kind of intimacy to occur in our lives, something more, much more, needs to happen because it is so unnatural for us. Fortunately for us, God never calls us to something without empowering and enabling its accomplishment. That is to say, after we have been invited to intimacy, the Holy Spirit remains beside us—and within us—to bring to fruition our yes to God. Jesus states in his prayer that he has glorified his Father, "by finishing the work you gave me to do" (John 17:4). This is how we glorify God: We do something that could not be done without him in our lives. We incline our hearts to the Father. We set our lives to this work he gives us: to be whole, intimate human beings.

Jesus appears to have a grand plan for us in his prayer, though not a predetermined plan set in mechanical detail into which we somehow have to fit. A plan such as that would not be a plan founded and rooted in relationship. In Jesus' plan he wants us to be intimate people so that his joy may be made complete in us (John 17:13). In a sense, "joy" is another name for God, the ground and source and foundation of all creation. God wants us to experience the joy that he is. This is not a joy bestowed after a lifetime of struggling to be intimate. This joy that is God seeps into our lives with the first moment of our coming to be and increases and surges forth with every "yes" to God. Sometimes in life that joy is experienced as a stream running full. At other times it is a single drop because it is a hard thing to live this way in the world. But there is always the joy, the constant and basic inner joy, of being about our Father's business.

The great and popular Christian apologist C. S. Lewis entitled his autobiography *Surprised by Joy*. The title has layers of meaning. Immediately, we think of Joy, his wife, who came like a surprise into his life. (If you haven't seen the movie *Shadowlands*, you simply must.) However, the book is *not* about his wife. Twenty years before he even met her, he had given the name *Joy* to the overwhelming longing that converted the atheist Lewis into a Christian. His experience of Joy, in both senses, was also mediated by God. God wants us to be joy-full—full of himself. And intimacy is essential for that to happen.

We propose that intimate friendship is essential to spiritual and psychological health. It is how we best come to know ourselves and God. He reveals himself to us through our relationships. It makes good sense to be prudent in our relationships. There are good reasons to place limits on how vulnerable we are with certain people. We are not called to indiscriminate intimacy. Yet neither can God have in mind for us a life constrained by disappointment, anger, or anxiety. He desires for us a life that enables us to flourish.

Discussion Questions

1. Are your spirituality and sexuality good friends, or like neighbors who converse infrequently, or outright enemies?
2. Have you ever considered how God views our sexuality?
3. What has been your understanding of intimacy?
4. What goes into an intimate friendship?
5. What enabled Mary to risk that kind of intimacy with Jesus?
6. Has God revealed himself to you through someone? In what ways?
7. Name moments of joy in your life. How did you feel? Can you see experiences of joy as experiences of God?

CHAPTER 2

Spirituality and Sexuality in Marriage

Here is a typical situation. A married couple experienced sexual difficulty. They were in their early thirties with small children. The wife felt that her husband wanted sexual intercourse too often. He felt rejected and frustrated. It was clear that they cared deeply for each other, and they functioned well together in other areas. They just needed some help in this matter. She related that when she was young, her older, teenage brother impregnated his girlfriend. Her parents were scandalized and forced her brother to get married. She recalled that thereafter her mother regularly reminded her of the dangers of being sexually active and bringing shame on the family. She said that even after being married, she still felt a little bit guilty about having sex. I shared some thoughts about what I see in scripture as God's attitude toward sexual intimacy between two people vowed to each other. She seemed intrigued by the idea that God means for us to give ourselves completely to each other and enjoy doing it. I also offered a possibility: She just might find a deeper giving of herself to God related to the sharing of herself with her husband.

With her present, I talked to him about the notion that sexual intimacy does not start in the bedroom. It starts when we wake up. It's in how we talk and listen to each other. It's in appreciation. It's in helping with the kids and household chores.

All of that is attractive and endearing. Sexual intimacy is a way of being together all the time; it isn't defined by intercourse alone. Kissing, conversation, embracing, and caressing are also forms of sexual intimacy. To have in mind that there is no sexual intimacy without intercourse is to deny ourselves the delight of all the ways of being close to our beloved.

Every therapist needs a couple like the one mentioned above for encouragement once in a while. They took to the ideas, put them in practice, and in short order they didn't need me any longer. It was a pleasure to work with them on the embrace of spirituality and sexuality in their relationship. It is our challenge and privilege as well.

GOD EXPRESSED, GOD RECEIVED

We state a premise here from which all other ideas in this chapter derive: In the relationship with our beloved we express and receive God. Let us consider these verses from Isaiah:

Do not fear, for you will not be ashamed;
   do not be discouraged, for you will not suffer disgrace;
for you will forget the shame of your youth,
   and the disgrace of your widowhood you will
      remember no more.
For your Maker is your husband,
   the LORD of hosts is his name;
the Holy One of Israel is your Redeemer,
   the God of the whole earth he is called.
For the LORD has called you
   like a wife forsaken and grieved in spirit,
like the wife of a man's youth when she is cast off,
   says your God.
For a brief moment I abandoned you,

but with great compassion I will gather you.
In overflowing wrath for a moment
    I hid my face from you,
but with everlasting love I will have compassion on you,
    says the LORD your Redeemer.

This is like the days of Noah to me:
    Just as I swore that the waters of Noah
    would never again go over the earth,
so I have sworn that I will not be angry with you
    and will not rebuke you.
For the mountains may depart
    and the hills be removed,
but my steadfast love shall not depart from you,
    and my covenant of peace shall not be removed,
    says the LORD, who has compassion on you.
      (Isa 54:4–10)

In this passage we see some of the shape and substance of a committed relationship. Absent are fear, shame, disgrace, humiliation, reproach, and lasting anger. In abundance are compassion, seeking for the other, kindness, peace, and unfailing love. God chooses to address himself to Israel, his people—you and me—through the language of the lover to the beloved. To be the lover and the beloved of someone is to take part in a redemptive, relational sacrament of God's making and indwelling. What we believe we know of our Lord is revealed, tested, and lived in committed relationship.

THE DILEMMA

Marriage is a crucible that exposes our reticence to give ourselves fully and our great need to do so. Moreover, it is a crucible in which we simultaneously engage our beloved and God. Our truest and best identity is found in giving ourselves to God, the source and the final end of our existing and so of our giving. Unfortunately, we are not inclined toward such a full offering of ourselves to God or to our beloved.

We seem to want to hold something of ourselves back, don't we? It is not, however, just pettiness on our part. There is something of an instinct for survival in it. Our ambivalence can make a case for itself. If we give ourselves completely to God and to our beloved, we are then completely vulnerable, aren't we? If we give all of ourselves and the relationship doesn't work out, we run the risk of being reduced to nothing. But if we set aside some portion of our mind and heart, we will have something of ourselves with which to start over again.

It's sobering to realize that nothing less than all of oneself is sufficient for real love, for love redemptive. One might think that giving nearly all should be adequate to make the relationship thrive. But it isn't. It seems that whatever we hold back does us in. My beloved says that she loves me, but I can't fully believe it because I haven't given her all of me to love. I tell her that I love her, but in all honesty, do I love her with all of myself? We withhold for the sake of psychological safety, yet it is our withholding that constrains the fulfillment of our vows, the flourishing of our relationship with God and our beloved. What we hold back is where our fears, doubts, depression, anger, discouragement, addictions, and anxiety take root. When we are unhappy in the relationship, we are acutely aware of what we are not receiving and often fairly oblivious to what we are not giving.

GIVING OUR SELF

My grandmother raised me until she died at the age of seventy; I was eight years old. Her memory is very dear to me. My uncle took me to visit her in the hospital, and it seemed that only a few months later I was at her graveside. Perhaps it was just how they did things back then. No one told me she was seriously ill. No one talked to me about her death. Life just went on. I went to live with my mother. There were some periods of tranquility in the midst of a great deal of instability. We moved a lot. My mother's romantic relationships were volatile. I remember her going voluntarily to the psychiatric hospital on two occasions for what was called a "nervous breakdown." When I was fifteen my mother wasn't able to take care of me any longer. I went to live in foster homes. I lived in three homes until I was eighteen. I think my foster parents did the best they could with me. But there was no way around the truth of it: I wasn't really their child, and their home wasn't really my home.

At age eighteen I was designated an emancipated minor by the court, which meant I was on my own. I went to university for a year. It was the Vietnam era and the draft was in effect. The lottery number I received assured that I would be drafted eventually, so I volunteered to go in early.

I met Nancy when we were in high school. We were still dating when I went in the army. She was in nursing school. We decided to get married. She was nineteen, I was twenty. The fact that no one in our wedding party was old enough to sign our marriage certificate as an adult witness should have told us something about what we were doing. But we loved each other. That's all we knew, and that was all we needed to know.

My background, however, caused her parents concern about what kind of husband I might be. Their concern, of course, was justified. Their daughter married a young man who was somewhat resourceful but lacked the emotional maturity to love her well and to accept her love. Through the first twenty years of life, with every loss, with every move to a new home, with every disappointment, I learned what it took to survive, to avoid unraveling. I understood without words that, at the end of the day, I could only count on myself.

Through more than three decades of marriage, through children and grandchildren, there is the ongoing challenge to respond with all of myself to her love, which is deep and wide. And it is the same challenge I have with God. The emotional survival skills that served me well through the early, tough times became liabilities in the presence of profound love. Without a doubt I wanted to love and be loved. The problem was that I couldn't give all of myself and set aside some piece of my heart for safekeeping.

I don't think I'm as guarded as I once was, though old ways die hard. But at least they are dying—by his grace. A sign of that grace is my experience of Nancy's love and God's love for me as interwoven. And it feels as though whatever I withhold of myself to her makes me less present to the Lord. The good news is that my response to God deepens with the giving of myself to her, and my response to her deepens with the giving of myself to God. This reinforces the fundamental conviction that while God is necessarily distinct from creation—and so from our human relationships—he is never separate from them. Our relationship with God is always mediated through our relationship with others.

YOU LOOK FAMILIAR

A good friend related a conversation with his sister. She had been in several romantic relationships. Most had been unsatisfying, with a few qualifying as downright nightmarish. She observed that for years she had been, figuratively speaking, dating her father. This was of interest to my friend, for he was sure he would have noticed such a development. She related that their father was not emotionally available to her, and the men she chose to date were eventually similar in that respect. She noted that she may have been trying to compensate for the relationship with her father by making a go of it with someone like him. A marvelous insight on her part, don't you think?

Sometimes we believe that our love is so strong that we have enough love to make up for what the other person is not giving. If this were so, there would be many more satisfied relationships. It takes two to dance, yet it becomes a melancholy embrace when our partner is not animated and does not wish to become so. The advice is common and sound: If we are hoping that our partner will change in some significant way after we are married, we are likely on a fool's errand. Marriage usually deepens what already exists in the relationship, for good or ill. If we want to rescue people, there are hundreds of worthy causes that will welcome our participation. We should not marry someone in spite of our personal misgivings, as we are likely to regret the choice.

For example, a young couple who had been dating for several years came for counseling about their relationship and their future together. She wanted to get married. She felt they had been going together long enough. Besides, a younger sibling was getting married before her, which just didn't seem right. He had recently been graduated from college and had his first job. He was enjoying being able to buy things after years of living on a student's budget and did not appear to share her urgency. They were asked about their view of their respective parents' marriages. I mentioned that I doubted that most marriages were 50/50 all the time in terms of how much each puts into the relationship. Given that, what percentage would they say they each put into their relationship? They looked at each other, seemingly searching for the other's answer before giving their own. She then said, "I would say that it's 80/20." She said this as evenly as if she were reading the weather forecast for tomorrow. I asked, "80/20 as in…?" "I put in 80 percent, he puts in 20 percent," she replied. She looked to him for his view. He stated good-naturedly, "I'd say that's about right."

I have to admit I hoped that hearing those numbers would startle them—that she would say, "I'm not marrying someone who only puts 20 percent into the relationship!" and that he would say with determination, "20 percent?! I've got to do better than that!" But they didn't. I don't know what they eventually decided about getting married. I do know that she deserved someone who would give more of himself. And he deserved someone to whom he was willing to give more than the minimum. Sometimes there are two good people who are not good for each other.

PLEASING GOD

Several years ago there appeared in our local newspaper a filler item, one of those snippets of information that editors use to complete a page. It stated that an employee of a prominent advertising company in our city would be taking an extended sabbatical from work to create a short film. As a young man he had wanted to become a filmmaker but couldn't find employment in the industry. He decided to take a job with this same advertising agency to learn film production skills until he could pursue his passion. A number of years passed. He never became a maker of films. He did, however, become a valued employee. The news item also stated that his company would continue to pay his salary while he was gone—which seemed generous.

A year or two later I happened to see another short item in the paper about this same fellow. He had finished his film. It was about a fictional order of monks who called themselves "The Clowns of God." Making God laugh was their charism, their purpose for being as a community. Judging by the description, to make God laugh they employed humor of the Monty

Python genre. The news item concluded by stating that this man who could now call himself a filmmaker had died from sudden illness.

I did not expect that ending to the story. Right away those two short items separated by more than a year came together. I imagined that he had received a grave diagnosis from his physician. He reflected on what he should do with the remainder of his life. He may have considered this piece of unfinished business from his youth, his desire to make films, and shared the somber news and his dream with his employer. Of course we don't know what really happened behind the scenes. It seems, though, he had only enough time to make one film. And he chose to tell a story about a group of people who decided that the most important thing they could do on this earth was to make God laugh, to make him happy, to please our Lord.

When, with sincere simplicity of heart, we seek to please our Father as our only motive, we are graced with his Spirit, set free from the demands of our self-seeking. We all have moments of such spiritual lucidity. How we wish those moments would become hours and days and a way of living all the time. But we fall back and we take control of our lives again and again. He waits for us to come to our senses and include him. But when we just want to please him for his own sake, we can feel our defenses fall away. We can and do accept his embrace peacefully. So the "Clowns of God" really were on to something. Seeking to please God is at the heart of spirituality. It is also at the heart of the relationship with our beloved.

PLEASING YOUR BELOVED

A pastor was sharing with a group his method of conducting premarital counseling. He would ask the man, "Why do you want to marry her?" The typical response would be, "Because she makes me happy." "Wrong answer!" the pastor would immediately counter. "You should want to marry her because you want to make *her* happy." This really is one of the hallmarks of strong couples: They maintain their desire to please each other. They take pleasure in seeing the other delighted. They anticipate the joy they will see in their beloved. It is good for us to be vigilant about this: "Do I still like to please my partner?" "When was the last time I surprised my beloved with an act of consideration, of generosity?"

It is difficult to overstate the value of this because marriages get better the same way they get worse—little by little. Small acts of love determine the direction of a marriage as surely as a rudder dictates the path of an ocean liner. And those small, steady offerings of love are often seen as more authentic evidence of positive change than the infrequent, grand gesture. God is indeed in the details of how we treat each other.

SPIRITUALLY

We please God and our partners when we support their relationship with our Lord. At the extremes we have heard of a husband pulling the sparkplug cables from the car to prevent his wife from attending "her" worship service. We have also heard spouses relate that their beloved has been nothing less than "a gift from God." There is no greater affirmation than for our partners to believe that their spirituality has been strengthened for having shared their lives with us. For better or worse we do have a significant influence on how welcome God is in our home. As one lady was reported to have said, "God makes it possible for me to go to heaven, but my husband has a lot to do with what kind of shape I'll be in when I get there."

The woman's comment underscores for us that it's impossible to be in good relationship with God without at least the ongoing attempt to be in good relationship with others. The vertical line to God, as it were, passes through—and never bypasses—the horizontal line of human relationships. The aforementioned husband has much to do with the woman's final destiny with God. That is true for all of us, married or celibate: Other people provide the formative matrix of our heavenly destiny.

EMOTIONALLY

What healthy and unhealthy couples have in common are problems. And problems we shall always have with us. But one of the important factors that characterize healthy couples is that they talk and listen to each other about their problems. There are no topics that are off limits. They are mutually respectful. They are not defensive. They stay on the topic under discussion without bringing in other topics and grievances to "make their case" (or to change the subject). Their motive in talking is not to prove who is right. What they are after is a consensus as to how they can solve the problem—or at least manage it more effectively. Sometimes there is no solution, and they just need to talk to each other.

This coincides—this talking and listening in genuine conversation—with how God approaches us in holy scripture. As Christians we believe that the scriptures are not to be thought of as a mere historical record of what happened a long time ago in far-off places. Rather, we believe God addresses us in these sacred words. And if he addresses us, if he talks to us, then the expectation is that we will listen and respond. In the early chapters of the Book of Genesis this is the paradigm of relationship between God and humankind. God creates by talking, by speaking: "And God *said*: 'Let there be...'" And once humankind has appeared in God's creative work, conversation—that is listening *and* speaking—becomes the vehicle of relationship. Perhaps we may say that all authentic human speaking and listening participates in this movement of the divine.

PHYSICALLY

There is a particular kind of magical thinking in regard to romantic relationships. That is, that our partners should know—without our having to say it—what pleases us physically. After all, that's how it's done in the movies. The lover seemingly intuits what the beloved most desires at just the right time. But the lover has the advantage of the soundtrack to signal that romance is imminent, and the script explains just what the lover should do. The rest of us have to tell each other what is pleasing. We have to push through embarrassment and awkwardness, and only then claim the joy of pleasing and being pleased by our beloved. We have to move past the notion that "good people" don't enjoy each other's bodies like a ripe peach on a summer's day. "Let your fountain be blessed, and rejoice in the wife of your youth, a loving deer, a graceful doe. May her breasts satisfy you at all times; may you be intoxicated always by her love" (Prov 5:18–19). Scripture does not lack for passages that celebrate lovers in communion. So let us communicate what pleases with respect and love.

Sometimes for Christians there is a dark element to their sexual experience, a suspicion that this experience in marriage, while immensely pleasurable, is somehow still not quite fully good. That suspicion flows from a complex of historical and psychological factors, and it must be countered. If God's holy creation includes all of us, wholly us, that necessarily includes our sexuality. The novels of Andrew Greeley, the Catholic priest-novelist-sociologist of the Archdiocese of Chicago, can be singularly helpful here. They show couples delighting and pleasuring one another, and encountering God in this experience, in the bond of marriage.

DATING FOR LIFE

One of the things we notice about couples whose problems are serious enough to come in for counseling is that they have quit dating. Dating is important, especially the longer we have been together. Couples will report that they used to go out regularly before they had so many responsibilities. It's as if dating is for the newly in love and a luxury the rest of us can't afford—literally and figuratively. But that's backwards: Dating is not a luxury for couples; it's a necessity. We have to make the time to be together. We have to insist on it since no one else is likely to insist on it for us. When we broach this topic with couples, some of them have reasons they can't go out regularly, such as: "We don't want to take time away from the children." It is a gift to children for their parents to date. Much of their security depends on the strength of their parents' relationship. Some couples say: "We can't afford it." There's little cost to a walk together in the park or at the mall. What we do on a date is really secondary to the fact that we are setting this time aside just for our beloved. We posit that we can't afford *not* to date. Dating strengthens and deepens our relationship. It is a tonic that wards off stagnation.

Healthy couples also maintain a sense of playfulness. The play between lovers is a delightful necessity that has its origin in our earliest relationships. It is part of a living stream of bonding love and friendship that begins in infancy and carries through the various stages of life. When a parent first nuzzles his or her infant's neck playfully and hears her laugh, heaven is present in the smile that passes between them. Is this not a holy moment? God is there in the occasion filling it with his presence—not God as a distant observer but God as the very love that passes between them. Adult lovers do not possess the innocence of an infant. But the play itself can still be innocent, delightful, and Spirit-filled.

Play is a serious matter to our well-being. The drive to refresh and recreate is innate. Playfulness must exist for us within our relationship with God as well or it will find its expression through illicit means. If our God is only the God of serious things, we will seek relief in distractions that are not of him. Being a couple with many obligations is somewhat like being a well from which buckets of water are drawn each day. Every well that refreshes others must have its own sources of refreshing. If not, the well eventually is drawn down to mud. That is when a couple is in trouble. Couples who date and who are playful with each other are refreshed by God's playfulness, by his indwelling in their love.

Discussion Questions

1. Do you know a couple who have a genuinely intimate way of being together?
2. What have you received of God in the person of your beloved?
3. How does it change us to believe that our relationship with God is lived out with our beloved?
4. How much of yourself have you risked in a relationship?
5. Does authentic love always carry a measure of risk?
6. What motivates us to commit ourselves to someone in spite of misgivings?
7. In what ways do you please God?

CHAPTER 3

Spirituality and Sexuality in Celibate Vocation

There are fundamental questions often implicit in discussions of celibacy: Can a celibate be a whole person in the way one can be who gives all of oneself to another? Or does the celibate, for the lack of that exclusive relationship, ultimately come up short in the full experience of intimacy with God and others? If we say that celibacy is at odds with adult intimacy, do we conclude that God has limited the full expression of himself to those in a monogamous sexual relationship? That would seem to make everyone else "children of a lesser God" in a crucial way, while placing a constraint on God's creativity to live within us and express himself through us—a constraint not found in scripture or in our experience of him.

The celibate is faced with a similar capacity for attraction as is the non-celibate. A group of seminarians was asked that if God gave them the choice, would they choose to be asexual, that is, normal in all other ways but not experience sexual attraction. One said that he would choose to be asexual because he would be much less distracted and better able to focus on his spirituality. That, of course, raises some fundamental questions about his understanding of spirituality. There are many different models or types of spirituality. Bookstores carry shelves full of every conceivable form of spirituality. However, the Christian tradition must insist upon an integrated spirituality. If some aspect of what it means to be human is omitted from this attempted integration, damage is done to the person, and dishonor is done to God. God, after all, is the source of all that makes us truly human. The remaining seminarians all gave reasons why they would not choose to be relieved of their capacity for attraction. One said that his sexuality makes him like others, which he wouldn't want to surrender. Another responded that contending with his sexuality gives him credibility with the people he will serve who also have to struggle with these issues in their lives.

AWARENESS

Sexuality consists of our thoughts, feelings, and behaviors in response to attraction. Sexual orientation speaks to the nature of our attraction: to which gender we are attracted and to what specific physical and personality traits. Another facet of our sexuality is how we evaluate ourselves for having a particular attraction. Do we feel good about it, guilty for having it, or neutral about the experience? Mature sexuality includes the ability to talk about our sexuality in an appropriate setting. Those conversations will necessarily differ in detail, given the context.

ORIENTATION

Numerous clients who identified their orientation as homosexual consistently described the process as one of discovering, of coming to a realization of their orientation as a young person or later in life. No one has recounted that he or she decided or chose to be attracted to their own sex. Clinical experience reflects the perspective of contemporary studies of sexuality: We do not appear to choose our orientation. Perhaps the analogy of appetite can be useful. I like watermelon. My wife likes watermelon. But one of our daughters does not. She did not like watermelon the first time we offered it to her as a toddler, and she does not like it to this day as an adult. Sexual orientation seems to be something like that. In spite of the overwhelming social messages that we should be attracted to the other sex, some are not. We are no more responsible for our sexual orientation than we are for liking or disliking watermelon. What we are responsible for is our sexual behavior. This is an absolutely key issue. Sexual orientation is not chosen but sexual behavior is.

Awareness of attraction and the ability to talk about it are indispensable to the formation of healthy adult sexuality. We need to be aware of our attractions generally, and specifically when we are with someone. Without that awareness we cannot guard the well-being of others or ourselves. We can deal with our attractions by denying we have them, ignoring them, and calling them by another name, or we can name our attractions honestly and accurately. In choosing that path we move in the grace-filled direction toward being capable of loving God and each other in an integrated fashion.

Although sexual contact is not present for the celibate, sexuality always is. If we were to make a list of the qualities we desire in a close friend, and a list of what we desire in a romantic partner, we would find a great deal of overlap: listening with genuine interest, empathy, affection, a sense of humor, and similar interests. This makes for a short distance between platonic friendship and romantic interest. Of course, there is the matter of physical attraction. It's interesting how much more attractive a person can become as we connect in other areas. There is always the potential for the unintended, unforeseen appearance of romantic attraction. It is an unavoidable occurrence, part of being an adult in relationship with other adults. Attraction is not a sign of moral failure or psychological defect. Rather, it is a sign of our humanity, of what we hold in common.

Genuine attraction calls for a mature response from the celibate. Many have come to useful knowledge about themselves in reflecting on what they brought to a relationship that resulted in attraction. The celibate gives a life affirming "yes" to God in contending with one's attraction with integrity and maturity.

INTIMACY

In the formation of mature sexuality, awareness is necessary both as a developmental marker and as a condition for the genesis of intimacy. Intimacy, or deep friendship, is knowing another and allowing oneself to be known. It is the foundation for authentic sexuality. Sexuality that is informed by intimacy does not diminish our capacity for attraction, but it does inform our attraction so that we may act in the best interest of the other. Without intimacy our sexuality gravitates toward mere self-gratification.

COMMITMENT TO INTIMACY

As we bring to mind those we have met who love generously, wisely, and well—being married is not what they have in common. Their similarity lies in the practical, indispensable way God informs how they relate to others. In the midst of contending with their own imperfections, they nonetheless possess the freedom to be loving, to know others, and to allow themselves to be known. We are called to be loving people. How that is lived may be as a married person or as a celibate in vocation. To be a healthy adult, an instrument of God's grace, requires a commitment to intimacy—to its value and possibility for us individually and corporately as the Body of Christ, his Church.

The resolve to be an intimate person involves a clear-eyed recognition that along with the joys of intimacy come miscues and misunderstandings. Our bias, however, is clear: Intimacy can be challenging and messy, but it is the only game worth playing. It is, in fact, God's game. He made us and calls us to relationship, to intimate friendship. The cost of playing is high, but the cost of sitting out is prohibitive.

There is no good reason for the celibate to be less committed to intimacy than the married person. If celibacy is practiced without the openness and the commitment to intimacy, the celibate loses something important. She or he, in the avoidance of intimacy, loses the graceful experience of vulnerability. Yes, vulnerability is a graceful experience. If the risk of being hurt or being misunderstood is entirely absent, then ongoing growth and maturation are largely constrained. For the Christian there is another dimension to this fact. Christians believe that in the birth and life of Jesus of Nazareth, God has become what we are, sin alone excepted. We have no completely open window into the human soul of Jesus. However, any fair reading of the gospels will show him reaching out in intimacy to others.

The celibacy of Jesus had absolutely nothing to do with misogyny. The gospels show him, especially the Gospel of St. Luke, having many women friends. He was not withdrawn; he was not a loner. It is true he had special alone times in prayer with his Father. It is no less true that he sought out companionship with others. In companionship with others, as we read in story after story in the gospels, he was intensely alive, full of joy, passionate, and compassionate. That such encounters were not intimate would be difficult to believe. Intimacy is not the same thing as sexual contact and sexual activity.

FAITHFULNESS

A monk related a winter weekend he spent with a few relatives and some of their friends. They rented a cabin with skiing as the main activity for the group. He was not a skier but brought along plenty of reading. The first morning everyone went skiing except him and a married friend of the family. They discovered they shared mutual interests. She was easy to talk to and a pleasure to be with. After several hours he recognized the beginning of a romantic interest on his part toward her. He said, "I began to wonder what it would be like to be married to her." Later, however, he recalled thinking, "Well, it doesn't matter because it would never work out. She's married and so am I."

To choose one good over another is an inherent aspect of love. To love God *and* others as a celibate or as a married person are both goods. In both vocations, one chooses and enters into a covenant relationship, a vow of faithfulness. The monk understood himself as "married" to his vocation. That understanding informed and oriented his behavior.

Making a vow to another is something of the utmost seriousness. It's something divine, we might say. A vow expressing absolute commitment, either as a married person or as a celibate person, mirrors God's absolute commitment to his creation. God's fidelity to his creation is forever. That's why vows are forever. They are, in that sense, divine.

MEETING YOUR NEEDS

Those we have met who live their celibacy well embrace the responsibility and privilege of meeting their needs by legitimate means. A young man comes to mind who expressed the realization that he was "tactile." He felt the need to embrace and be embraced in platonic friendship. He said that attitudes toward the clergy made that more difficult than in previous eras. He reluctantly concluded that he would probably just have to get used to life without much physical affirmation. I asked if he had ever had a therapeutic massage. He replied that he had not and was hesitant to do so. We talked about it a bit more and moved on to other matters. The next time I saw him he had been to a massage therapist and planned to go again. He remarked, once he got past the initial awkwardness, how affirming it was to be touched in a non-sexual way. This was particularly important to him, since he had been sexually abused as a boy. This is a good example of meeting a genuine need authentically.

Dealing with loneliness—the need for companionship—is often an issue in celibacy. We recognize this as a significant challenge to the abundant life Christ came to give us. It seems particularly incumbent upon the diocesan celibate to create family. One's family of origin may not live close by or the family may be sufficiently toxic as to discourage regular contact. We are born into one family, but as adults we get to choose the members of a second one.

The formation of a second family is a lifelong endeavor of love, necessity, and opportunity. It is essential for the celibate to "own" this process. I recall a fellow who was working and living at a parish. He was not able to go home for Thanksgiving that particular year. I asked what he was going to do. "I'm hoping a friend or one of the parishioners will invite me over for dinner," he replied. I wondered aloud how they would know to offer the invitation. He smiled and I smiled because we both knew that he wanted to be invited without having to let it be known that he was available for the holiday. That's so like us, isn't it? We wish for others to meet our needs without having to appear that we have any. It would be nice if it worked, but so often it doesn't. We honestly don't have grounds for being hurt or resentful when someone hasn't responded to a need we have not clearly communicated. Hoping that others will intuit our need and seek us out is the stuff of magical thinking.

Real life requires the proactive formation and nurturing of healthy friendships. Providing companionship to others and seeking them out when you need them is how adults relate to one another. There is a toast that reflects the result of gathering a family of friends: "We are grateful for family who are like friends and friends who are like family." The celibate who practices intimacy with just such a family of friends avails him or herself of a sanctuary for the seasons of their life. We need people in our life with whom we do not have to pretend that we are doing better than we really are. Reciprocal, healthy, intimate friendship—this is what the unity prayer of Jesus in John 17 looks like as a lived experience.

Discussion Questions

1. Jesus the celibate performed one of his earliest miracles on behalf of a newly married couple. Is there a message in this for us?
2. What do you need from others to support your choice of celibacy?
3. How did your expectations of celibacy compare with the reality of living it?
4. How can you tell when platonic friendship takes on aspects of romantic interest?
5. How do you respond when you are attracted to someone?
6. Do you see yourself as committed to intimacy?
7. Have you set some intimacy need aside for the sake of being celibate?
8. How are your abilities in the area of forming and nurturing a second family?

CHAPTER 4

Spirituality and Sexuality for Singles

I'm impressed with the importance of practicing the "right now" of God in my life: a readiness to receive him and express him to others just as my life is at this moment—a spirituality from the inside out. I would like to present myself to him as a much better person than I am, but I need him first—at this very moment—in my life. I need to enter his life in my present, scruffy condition. The model many of us grew up with doesn't work in this instance. It won't do for me to try and clean up my house before I invite God in. I need him right now; otherwise, I'll remain scruffy and my house unclean in the same ways indefinitely.

The "right now" of being single presents the question of how that relates to one's spirituality. Some experience the lack of a romantic companion as an impediment to their spirituality; others see it as an advantage to relate to God without the many distractions of marriage. For the purpose of our discussion, we note three groups of singles in regard to how they view their status: (1) Those who are content and committed to being single; (2) Those who are not content with being single while they wait for a partner; and (3) Those who are content with being single but open to being in a committed, romantic relationship.

CONTENT AND COMMITTED TO BEING SINGLE

Singles in this group have the stability of living in the present as they intend to live in the future. They experience attraction without the idea that mutual attraction might someday become marriage. And because this is so, it is only fair for committed singles to inform early on the person with whom there is mutual attraction of their resolve to remain single. In so doing they make plain the inherent limits in the relationship. It is unkind, to say the very least, to accept someone's deepening love, all the while knowing we will allow that person only so far into our lives.

As for their spirituality, singles in this group are free to respond to God just as they are. They encounter and express God's love in their relationships with close family and friends. And God is quite capable of truly, fully making himself known in the midst of those intimate bonds. There is no "less than" in their relationship with God as a single, for there are no second class citizens in the kingdom of God (Gal 3:26–29). To claim him as Lord is to avail ourselves of his creative, redemptive, and passionate love for us. God does not have a version of himself for singles and one for married people.

We discern a way to live that makes sense in light of our needs, preferences, temperament, and experiences. If we come to the conclusion that being single is the best way to live, and we want to love God as a single person, he is willing and able to fill that way of life in full measure with himself. We know this because Jesus is the model par excellence for the committed single.

Jesus said that he came to give us the abundant life (John 10:10). And in many instances he showed us the full life he has with the Father in the quality of his friendships, the life he means for us to have with him and with others through him.

Being single or married are choices available to us; being an intimate human being is not an option in the abundant life. Without intimate friendship, our experience of God remains largely abstract—untested, unknown, and dull.

The life that Jesus, as a single person, shared with God is the very same eternal love affair that he offers to committed singles. There is no diluted quality to the working of the Holy Spirit in one's life as long as the resolve to remain single is not a retreat from the rewarding, frustrating, unpredictable, and absolutely life-affirming vocation of intimate friendship. Henri Nouwen said that there is not a cup of joy and a cup of sorrow for us to drink from in this life. There is only one cup with joy and sorrow mingled. This is the cup we drink from. We, sustained by the Spirit of Christ, drink from the cup in our commitment to being single and being an intimate friend.

NOT CONTENT AS A SINGLE

It's a particularly troublesome place to be in our spirituality when we are unhappy and have determined that we will remain unhappy until God or somebody changes our circumstances. And that, unfortunately, is the central difficulty for us when we conclude that contentment cannot be ours until we have a romantic partner.

There is a demand in this stance that seems to say to God, "You *will* bless me as a married person or not at all." There doesn't seem to be much room in this for God's leading because we have decided (for us and for God) under what condition God will affirm us. The implicit message to God in this position is that we cannot be content because he has not given us enough—or he himself is not enough for us.

As for the person who might become our beloved, if we were never content as a single and looked to a romantic relationship as the solution to our discontent, he or she would come into the relationship bearing the burden of our unrealistic expectations.

The truth of the matter is that, if we do not feel close enough to God as a single person, being married is not the solution. And if we have not been able to form deeply rewarding friendships as a single, getting married won't solve that either. Those deficits in maturity, attitudes, and skills that keep us from being consistent and stable in our friendship with God and others will not be addressed by the act of marriage. What is likely is that our intimacy problems will show themselves all too soon in marriage. The most favorable circumstance for marriage is for it to be a continuation and deepening of one's capacity for spiritual, physical, and psychological intimacy.

We are best prepared spiritually and psychologically for marriage when we have developed sufficiently so that being married becomes a preference rather than a demand, when it is something we want but do not need to feel worthwhile and capable of intimate friendship with God and others.

In fact, most of us know singles who would make great partners. They love the Lord, they are remarkable friends to us, and they want very much to share their lives in marriage. And we, who are blessed by their presence in our lives, are perplexed as to why such wonderful people are not already married, since they are so well qualified and want to be married. It really doesn't seem fair. And the unfairness of it overwhelms our friends sometimes. We try to console them with our friendship and wonder to ourselves what deal we can make with God if only he would send them the person they deserve. Often we feel inadequate to console them and a bit guilty, too, if we already have our beloved. We are left to add our friends' unwanted singleness to that expansive list of situations we cannot control.

If we are that single person, there is the uncertainty of how and when and if we will meet the person that God has in mind for us. In response to that uncertainty, some singles are fairly assertive in their search; they are socially active with the idea that they are increasing their chances of meeting their intended. Other singles have decided to live their lives within its natural rhythm. They believe that God is well capable of arranging the introduction in his time and way.

What is important, however, in response to the uncertainty, is to not allow it to define us. And that is no small task. The fact that we are single and want to be married is important, but how important is it in defining ourselves? Perhaps a visual exercise will help with the answer.

Take a sheet of paper. Think of what is important about you and to you. For example, your relationship with God, your friends, and family; what you do for a living or would like to do; how you feel about yourself; how you look; and that you are single and want to be married. Now, with all the honesty within you, draw each item you noted as a circle on the paper, with the size of the circle reflecting how important that issue is in your life right now.

What some of us are likely to see is that wanting to be married has taken on an importance that eclipses other relationships and issues. It is not pleasant to see that my "wanting to be married" circle is larger than my "relationship to God" circle—but it is sobering and instructive. It suggests that perhaps our singleness has come to dominate and define us. And that is well worth addressing with courage and God's grace. For it is entirely possible for us to want a change of circumstance in our life without allowing that desire to deny us the quiet, deep joy of being content.

CONTENT AND OPEN

If contentment is having everything we want, then contentment, if we are to have it at all, becomes an infrequent, fleeting experience. Contentment becomes a way of living, however, if we believe that contentment is having what we need, and those needs are informed by our relationship with God.

We take possession of authentic power in believing and saying, "God knows my strong preference to be married. But right now this is the life I have, and it is a good one. I have the love of my Lord. I have people to love and who love me. I give myself to this life and I allow this life to give itself to me. I will not sit at the bus stop of life waiting to be married. It will happen or it will not happen. I choose to live right now."

This is a hopeful and realistic way to live. It prevents us from being taken hostage by something we cannot control. We decline turning a preference into a need whose absence defines us. In claiming our contentment in the present, we avoid being wounded by disappointment, which can become spiritual estrangement.

RUTH

She is a powerful, poignant illustration of someone who was content to be single, yet open to being married. In the book of the Bible bearing her name, we see that her devotion to Naomi, her mother-in-law, was not required of her. The death of her husband and the lack of a prospective husband within Naomi's immediate family gave Ruth the right to return to her own people. Her love for Naomi, however, superseded other considerations. She and Naomi were financially destitute and forced to relocate. The future was uncertain and yet Ruth was content. She was content because she had what she needed, and her needs were informed by her love for God. Ruth's contentment was such that one could easily imagine a parallel story without remarriage in which she and Naomi lived out their days sustained by their friendship with God and each other.

It's not surprising that the words of deeply devoted friendship spoken by Ruth to Naomi (1:16–17) are sometimes used in marriage ceremonies:

> Do not press me to leave you
> or turn back from following you!
> Where you go, I will go;
> where you lodge, I will lodge;
> your people shall be my people
> and your God my God.
> Where you die, I will die—
> there will I be buried.
> May the LORD do thus and so to me,
> and more as well,
> if even death parts me from you!

Ruth's words are, in the larger context, God's words to us individually and collectively: He will always be with us; he will never leave us. His commitment to us is not negotiable. Ruth's immortal proclamation of devotion strikes a universal chord. Her words mirror the depth of love we have (or want to have) for our Lord, for our children, a sibling, parent, friend, or spouse. To love like that is to be profoundly content, to be in possession of true, lasting treasure.

Boaz, her eventual husband, must have noted that contentment in Ruth. It made her beautiful. Ruth was a loving person and was loved. In her humble way she carried that knowledge like royalty. Boaz was attracted to her contentment. She did not need him because God had provided for her needs; but she was open to marriage.

A PARTNER IN FAITH

A great deal of the attraction of Boaz for Ruth must have been that he was a man of faith. She would not have to explain or justify her love for the Lord to him, since he understood out of his own life of devotion. This is a central issue in the decision to go forward in a romantic relationship. If he or she is antagonistic or even indifferent to our relationship with God, that is going to play out continually in our day-to-day life together. How we spend our time and money, our values, how we want our children to be raised—all of these priorities are likely to become points of contention. And in fairness, if we knew that he or she did not share our faith going into the relationship, do we really have the right to expect that person to change on such an important matter?

We realize that life and love are full of compromises. That is most certainly the case in marriage. We don't always get what we want or give what is desired of us. We are not suggesting that everyone hold out for the person who is a perfect match in the area of spirituality. But there are very real consequences for every degree of separation that exists between spouses in their commitment to a relationship with God. We need to be clear-eyed about that. If we decide that he or she has so many other admirable qualities that it makes being together worthwhile—so be it. But that decision should take into account that the differences in spirituality between the two of you are likely to be an ongoing source of tension.

Also, a prospective partner should not encourage or require us to abandon healthy relationships with friends or family as the price of being together. The suggestion that a romantic relationship is served by excluding those who love us speaks of insecurity and of immature affection.

Excluding others may also reveal an aspect of narcissism. One medieval thinker, Richard of St. Victor, had a superb insight. He maintained that there was a real danger of destructive narcissism in a relationship between two lovers: They may see only each other. Indeed, for all kinds of reasons, they may see only the "self" in the eyes of the other—that is, unless their relationship is open to include "an other."[1] Richard calls this other the *condilectus*, Latin for "the one loved along with the other." This perspective speaks to a generosity and creative inclusiveness in relationships of true love.

Of additional concern is that emotional or physical abuse is often preceded by isolating one's partner from their sources of spiritual and psychological support. A straightforward litmus test for the relationship is to ask ourselves if this is the kind of person we would want for someone else we love. Is this someone similar to whom we would want our child, sibling, or best friend to commit their life to? If in all honesty we hesitate to answer yes, it has much to say about our own answer.

SINGLE PARENTS

The integration of spirituality, intimacy, and sexuality for those who are single, and particularly for single parents, is of personal interest. Nancy and I have two daughters who have been single parents. We witnessed the joy and frustration sometimes in the same hour, and the just plain hard work of being a single parent. They had to be mom *and* dad, work during the day *and* attend to their children the rest of the time—all of which they did without the support, solace, or companionship of a spouse. The marriages ended but the needs of the children and their own needs did not. The life of a single parent is certainly not glamorous, but it *is* heroic in its impact on the children.

This is the part that is added into the choice of a partner for single parents. What kind of person will he or she be as a parent to my children? Are they tolerated because they are mine, or is there a genuine interest in them, a concern for their well-being?

Before John married our daughter Sarah, he asked to have lunch with me. He wanted to assure me of his deep love for her, of his commitment to being a good husband. He also said that in marrying Sarah he was committing himself to loving and caring for our granddaughter Isa as well. John has been more than good to his word. Sarah has a good husband; Isa has a good daddy; and Nancy and I are blessed. We desire this blessing for every single parent.

Single parents and their children need our love and support. The interest and practical help we offer them has a meaning and importance beyond the immediate benefit, which is important enough. I didn't realize until many years later how much my understanding of God was shaped by the encouragement and help of adults when I was a youngster. There were neighbors, teachers, baseball coaches, Boy Scout leaders, church family—all of them spoke to me with a common voice, now that I look back on it. They said, "You are worth something; we like you; you will have a good life; use your gifts." And, just as important, their collective presence told me that I was not alone. And when you don't have a dad around, that means a lot.

Perhaps that is why, of all the promises in scripture, the one I cling to most is, "And remember, I am with you always, to the end of the age" (Matt 28:20). It is the one promise I cannot do without. All those adults helped me form a belief, a faith in God as the one who is always right here with me. Even when I'm most discouraged I know it to be true. I may not feel it at the moment, but I know it is true.

SINGLE BUT NOT ALONE

I wish I could say that one of the benefits of being married is that we never feel alone. Pastors, spiritual directors, and counselors are accustomed, however, to hearing the painful admission that the companionship of marriage has devolved into isolation and aloneness. Consequently, many married people and singles know the feeling of being alone. And, above all, the idea that we are ultimately alone is the lie we must summon courage, passion, and the grace of God to refute. We have never been alone, we are not alone, and we will never be alone. What is the use of God if he is not, above every attribute, who he says he is—with us and in us and in each other? There is nothing that contradicts the assertion of our essential aloneness like the truth of intimate friendship. We must pray for it, work at it, and fight for it—fight the temptation to flee from the cost of being vulnerable and transparent. The reward is that intimacy is redemptive: The giving and receiving of it makes us whole.

INTIMACY SKILLS

We use the word often. We are counseled to have it in our lives. But what is intimacy made of? With regularity over the years we notice recurring skills present in deep friendship. In the following three chapters we offer six skills: commitment, transparency, boundaries, affirmation, accountability, and forgiveness. The practice of these skills is integral to friendship with God, with self, and with others.

Discussion Questions

1. Is there anything preventing you from practicing the "right now" of God in your life?
2. As a single, to which of the three groups do you belong?
3. What do you wish your married friends understood about you as a single?
4. What is in your cup of joy and sorrow?
5. Is there something keeping you from being content?
6. Has there been a time when a problem or situation defined or dominated you?
7. Could you be content and single the rest of your life?
8. Which spiritual values and practices would there need to be agreement on between you and a potential spouse?

CHAPTER 5

Commitment

COMMITMENT

There is a certain commitment to every human person whose path we cross, not profound or deep, but nevertheless real. It is the fundamental willingness to be there in response to the other's need. The Jewish philosopher, Emmanuel Levinas, has a wonderful phrase to express it: "Here I am! What can I do to help?"[1] That basic level of ethical commitment seems demanded in virtue of being human. But, of course, there is so much more to commitment than that. Deep commitment does not ordinarily occur at the beginning of a friendship. It is too important and its consequences too far reaching to offer to a person who may become no more than an acquaintance. Yet, it must of necessity come into play for a friendship to become genuinely intimate. Most of us have probably misjudged at one time the degree of mutual commitment that existed in a friendship. It surprised us how little it really took to end a relationship we thought to be fairly solid. It can be a source of confusion, anger, and/or sadness.

Commitment must be present for friendship to survive both the push-and-pull of everyday life and the crises that put relationships to the test. For the sake of clarity, we speak here of commitment as the resolve to maintain a healthy relationship. We feel obligated to place this parameter on the topic to avoid the problems inherent in the extreme. In speaking of intimate friendship, we have in mind safety and also at least the willingness to learn how to respond positively to the other. We certainly have the right to commit ourselves to whomever we choose, no matter how unhealthy or unsafe the situation. We presuppose here, however, a basic level of safety and health in the relationship. In this chapter we consider God's commitment to us, our commitment to him, commitment to ourselves, and commitment in intimate friendship.

GOD'S COMMITMENT

My mother and I live 1200 miles apart. A few years ago, prior to one of my visits, I called as usual to remind her that I would be there in two days. When I arrived at her residence, she was not in the lobby waiting as she normally is. I asked an employee of the residence if my mom had come down yet. With a disapproving look, he replied that she had been in the lobby all the previous day waiting for me. Consequently, on the next visit a few months later I decided to arrive unannounced to avoid a similar misunderstanding.

I went to her room, but she wasn't there. I asked one of the staff where I might find her. She said that perhaps she was still in the cafeteria. As I entered I saw my mother seated across the room at a round table alone with her back to me. I took a seat next to her and casually turned to face her. She looked at me calmly while I waited for her to speak, which she did not. I smiled and asked, "Do you know who I am?" She continued to look at me and replied, "I don't believe I do." I could see it was true. I said, "I'm your son, John." She continued to look at me for a few more seconds. She then tapped her forehead with her hand and stated enthusiastically, "Of course you are!" A few days later on the plane returning home I was surprised by a wash of emotion. My mother had forgotten who I was. Intellectually, I understood it as Alzheimer's disease. Emotionally, though, it was hard to accept that anything could cause her to forget her own son. There was another facet, however, to my response. Shortly before coming to visit my mother I had given a talk. One of the verses I chose to read was Isaiah 49:15: "Can a woman forget her nursing child, or show no compassion for the child of her womb? Even these may forget, yet I will not forget you." Seated in that plane, I felt the loss and God's promise together.

That is God's commitment to us: He will not forget us. We are always remembered, always on his mind. It is constantly true, even when despair or tragedy make it difficult to breathe, much less believe. It is so true that it perseveres even when we are left with little capacity to experience it or have faith in it. There is more to God's commitment, however, for his is not a passive remembering from a distance. We are never forgotten, never abandoned, because he is at all times beside us and within us (Matt 28:20; John 14:17). And he is actively working for our good. "For surely I know the plans I have for you, says the Lord, plans for your welfare and not for harm, to give you a future with hope" (Jer 29:11). God desires a constant intimacy with us, one in which he enfolds us within himself—yet in such a fashion that we are never suffocated, never diminished, but simply flourish within his embrace.

For one who is responding to God's ever-present invitation to intimacy, the ordinary things of the world take on a gift-like aspect. Nature, other persons, experiences of beauty, truth, and goodness—even occasions of suffering and pain not sought after but named and accepted—the entirety of existence becomes a gift to be accepted.

OUR COMMITMENT TO GOD

Our relationship to God is informed by a tension between two conditions. The first is succinctly stated in Isaiah 55:8–9: "For my thoughts are not your thoughts, nor are your ways my ways, says the Lord. For as the heavens are higher than the earth, so are my ways higher than your ways and my thoughts than your thoughts." God is beyond our finite understanding. The second condition is beautifully related in the first three chapters of Genesis. Of all creation, God made us in his image. He also made sure that Adam and Eve had each other for companionship. God kept company with them as well. Genesis begins and Revelation ends with humanity living in intimate friendship with our Creator in paradise. Our Lord is at once far beyond our comprehension and calling us to companionship with him. Given this state of affairs, what response, what commitment can we put our hearts to with God?

One of our favorite scenes in scripture is found in the thirty-second chapter of Genesis. Jacob has sent everything he owns and all of his family across the river. It is night. He camps alone by the river, anticipating the encounter that awaits him with his estranged brother in the days to come. But he is not alone, after all. A man takes hold of Jacob. And he, in self-defense, takes hold of the man in a struggle that lasts throughout the night. At some point Jacob realizes that he is wrestling with God himself. God is ready to end the encounter, but Jacob, in great need of courage to face his brother, refuses to let go without a blessing. Jacob contends with God and is changed by it. God renames him "Israel" to mark their encounter. God also gives him a limp as a reminder of who really is the better wrestler.

This is what we commit to God: our resolve to contend with him, to engage him always. This commitment to God is a particular manifestation of devotion. Resolving to take hold of

God is devotion born of our great need for, and hope in, our Savior. God can handle our anger, confusion, or despair—even when it is directed towards him. Of greater concern is when we allow ourselves to become indifferent to him. That is a particularly worrisome state to be in. We should take hold of God in urgent times. Instead, we often pull away from him when it feels as though he has let us down or abandoned us. "How could he let this happen to me or my loved one?" God says, "Take hold of me. I may not give you what you want, but I will give you what you need—myself, my very Spirit within you." To paraphrase William Barclay, we do well to remember that Jacob could never have taken hold of God without God taking hold of him first. It is God who makes our commitment to him possible.

COMMITMENT TO OURSELVES

It may sound selfish, even odd, to speak of "commitment to ourselves." Yet, we really can't function as whole people without it. It is part of the work that is necessary to the integration of spirituality, intimacy, and sexuality in our lives. It simply won't do to exempt ourselves from the practice of commitment. For example, some people of faith have a tendency to maintain two sets of standards, one for others and one for themselves. We see this play out in their tolerance and compassion for others who have erred, virtues that they deny themselves. They are disarmingly forthright about how it works, and to them it seems entirely natural to operate this way. They relate that when others err they should not be judged harshly. Hopefully, they will acknowledge their wrong, seek forgiveness, learn something from the experience, and move forward with God's blessing. For themselves, however, a similar mistake has more serious consequences. They should know better than to have done that—it is inexcusable. Therefore, they should suffer self-reproach for a long time. They also report that even after receiving forgiveness, it is difficult to let go and forgive themselves for failing God. Does this sound familiar to you? It does to us because we pass through it ourselves.

We are led to the conviction that an essential piece of a healthy commitment to ourselves includes the application of one set of values. There is a straightforward, though not easy, way to orient ourselves to this practice. Take your mistake, your sin. Imagine that it belongs to a friend. Is she a bad person for having fallen? How should she perceive herself? How does God feel about her? Should she, can she, accept God's forgiveness as the last word on the matter? Does she have your love and support? Apply all your answers to your own situation. Repeat as necessary.

We use self-deprecation to make ourselves do the right thing, to keep ourselves doing the right thing, and to punish ourselves when we fail to do the right thing. It is a harsh path, unhealthy and unnecessary. We appreciate that people take their relationship with God seriously and want to give their best. But no matter how noble the intent, there is something inherently unsavory and contradictory in flailing ourselves into the embrace of the Father. We can hold ourselves accountable while being compassionate and loving—toward others *and* ourselves. In fact, we glorify God in doing so.

Our tendency to disparage ourselves arises in many instances from unrealistic expectations. When I was about sixteen years old, flooded with hormones and uncertainty, I thought about how good it would be when I reached forty—then I would have things figured out. The problem is that every stage of life brings another set of things to figure out. We never seem to run out of problems with which to contend—about ourselves, about others, about God. Our experience is that God has been and is patient with us in this process of growing in his likeness.

Some express a concern that they will become spiritually complacent if they are less impatient with themselves, less disparaging. It seems to them to be a spiritual necessity to hold themselves to a higher standard than they use for others. We find, however, that those who are most concerned about becoming spiritually complacent are among the least likely to become so.

What we desire is the experience of being content, which is a very different thing from being complacent. Spiritual complacency carries the veneer of spirituality but is, at heart, pride in one's self-sufficiency. God does not have much to do in this instance. Spiritual contentment comes from God and is sustained by God. As William Barclay wrote, "We could never even have sought him unless he had already found us."[2] And having found us, we can be "confident of this, that the one who began a good work among you will bring it to completion by the day of Jesus Christ" (Phil 1:6). Our contentment results from confidence in God. He is in charge of this process of change. He is always ahead of us.

We can be content because God is already loving us with all the love he has to give. He is not waiting for us to become different in some way to love us more. God couldn't wait for us to become perfect to start loving us, so he began loving us just as we are. For how could we ever begin to change without first having his love? It is God who enables us to appropriate his love and return that love in friendship. Citing St. Augustine, the *Catechism of the Catholic Church* puts it well: "God thirsts that we may thirst for him" (2560). God is quite simply passionate about us, and not "us" in some generic way, but you and me specifically and particularly.

COMMITMENT IN FRIENDSHIP

Committed friendship is nurtured by a reasonable, realistic perspective that recognizes that we simply are not capable of meeting each other's expectations all the time. Because we are imperfect, we inevitably fail at some point to be the person our friend needs us to be. Yet, for that very reason, we terminate friendships that could become much better ones. We imagine that there are friends who are so attuned to each other that they do not experience conflict. They are lucky and rare. The rest of us have to contend with the push and pull of trying to be the kind of friend God is to us without the natural propensity to do so. We are often disappointed because we implicitly expect perfection from a friend—a perfection that we are not ourselves equipped to offer in return.

A committed friendship also possesses a certain robustness, an ability to endure those things that go wrong between us. This robustness is a lived-out belief that the relationship supersedes particular grievances. Similar to our commitment, our devotion to God, this is a taking hold of each other in friendship. It is a mutual act of human assent and divine grace to sustain the friendship in the face of our inability to give ourselves perfectly to it.

Belief in the primacy of the relationship also fosters the resolve to refrain from unilateral decisions. We can all recount more than one instance in which a friend suddenly stopped talking to us. We wondered what happened, what we said or did to provoke such a change. We can probably assume that there was a perceived provocation and that the other person decided to terminate the friendship without talking to us about it—a unilateral decision. Commitment to friendship entails resisting the temptation to cut the other person off in response to being wounded. It is a natural and powerful temptation. It feels entirely necessary at the time. The problem is that we survive psychologically by doing this, but at a loss to our maturation.

Our growth as mature adults capable of intimate friendship depends on this process of engaging the friend who has offended us. It is where we learn about ourselves *and* each other. We come to see our limits and potential. We encounter a depth of generosity in ourselves and in the other person that surprises us. We sometimes come to see how an issue from our past has carried forward into the present. This leaves us with the choice to contend with the issue or allow it to derail our friendships. This is the hard work of being a friend—to be like Jesus and seek the very one who has failed you. It changed St. Peter forever, and it changes us.

Discussion Questions

1. Has there been a time when you sensed God's invitation to intimacy?
2. Is there something intimidating about the prospect of intimate friendship with God?
3. Has there been a time when God's commitment to you was tangible, or a time when you felt the absence of his commitment to you?
4. In what ways does the lack of intimate friendship with others hinder our relationship with God?
5. Are you harder or more lenient on yourself than you are with others?
6. Can we be spiritually content yet still aware of how we need to grow?
7. How robust are you as a friend?
8. What do you expect of a close friend?
9. How are your abilities in the areas of seeking out the friend who has offended you or responding to being told you have been hurtful to another?

CHAPTER 6

Transparency and Boundaries, Affirmation and Accountability

TRANSPARENCY

When we speak of transparency in the context of intimate friendship, we have in mind behavior that is consistent with what we are thinking and feeling. It is transparency that is intentional. There is the freedom to be authentic in a friendship that is mutually transparent. It does not, however, come naturally for many of us. We are conditioned to act as though we are fine even when we are not.

When asked how she is doing, a client may respond that she is doing fine even though she appears anxious or depressed. I may offer, "Maybe you're not feeling well or you're tired, but your eyes tell me that you're not fine." Many fruitful conversations have begun from that point. Our eyes speak the truth with a constancy that our words can only envy.

The first order of business with transparency is to become transparent to ourselves. Naming and owning what is going on inside is useful, though sometimes uncomfortable. In fact, we notice a strong correlation between how important an issue is for our growth and our discomfort in addressing it.

One potential opening toward transparency begins, for instance, when we are confused by our response to an event. We may be confused because our response was less or more intense than we expected.

Here is a personal example. A number of years ago I made the decision to legally change my last name to that of my mother's family. I never had a relationship with my birth father. I saw him twice, both times by my initiative. The first time was when I was seven or eight years old. The conversation may have lasted two minutes. I went to see him at the garage where he worked, which must have been uncomfortable for him. The second time I talked to him I was in my thirties, with a family of my own. I visited the little town where I was born, where he still lived. I called his home and asked to speak to him. I told him that I was in town and would like to talk with him for a few minutes. He came to the restaurant where I was. We talked for about fifteen minutes. I had some questions for him about his relationship with my mother. She had always evaded my questions on the subject. I suspected that I was the result of a brief affair. He confirmed that was the case. He was forthright with me, which I greatly appreciated. Afterward, I stepped outside with him. We shook hands and said good-bye. It seemed to me that we would never see each other again. There was no need to. We had our own lives. It had always been that way. I watched him walk down the sidewalk. About thirty yards away he turned and waved good-bye.

It was a few years after that meeting that I decided to change my name. I was working towards my doctorate. It didn't seem right to have the name of a person on my diploma who was essentially a stranger. It was my family, the people named Galindo, who raised me and loved me and helped me on my way. The legal process was straightforward. I paid a small fee and placed a notice of my name change in a designated place in the county courthouse. I don't remember the reason for it, but at least two more times at some interval I had to replace the old notice with a new one. On the appointed day, I went to the courthouse to take the notice down for the last time. I went to the clerk's office. The notice was taken to a judge to sign. The clerk returned the notice to me. It was official. I was Galindo.

It was a sunny day, as I recall. I was happy—quite happy, actually. I was walking downtown and stopped for an ice cream to eat on the way. As I continued walking, however, I became sadder and sadder, which really confused me. I had no idea what this was about, and I needed to know. It was as if I was standing beside a rope that went under a closed door. I picked up the rope, walked to the door, and opened it—only to find that the rope continued to another door a few yards away. With each door I opened I became sadder. It felt odd to be walking down a busy sidewalk in the middle of the day while visualizing this. When I got to the last door I stopped walking because I felt uncomfortable with so many people around. I opened the door and there it was, the source of my unexpected response: I had been carrying around a pilot light of hope that someday my birth father would call. He would say that it was a mistake not to have been involved in my life, and that he wanted us to be good friends. By the act of changing my name, I was affirming that his call was never going to come. I was sad because I was experiencing the death of a hope I had unknowingly carried in my heart. With this matter, at least, I became transparent to myself.

To be transparent to oneself, to be self-aware, requires the ability to identify and tolerate contradictory emotions that often exist simultaneously. This is particularly difficult for some of us. We deal with the dilemma by denying that one of the emotions exists, perhaps naming it something other than what it really is. Sometimes we convert the emotions into a physical complaint in order to avoid experiencing them directly. In fairness, it is a lot to take in that you love someone who behaves in a way that alienates you—or that you don't love someone you feel like you're supposed to love. There are also contradictions about ourselves to contend with: that we desire intimate friendship but realize we are afraid of it, or that we are really not able to tolerate as much intimacy as we say we would like to have with others. It seems, however, that this experience of conflicted emotions is common to us all.

We do not let transparency come to fruition when we pass judgment on ourselves for our mixed feelings. We ask, "How can I love God and be angry with him at the same time?" When our answer to that question is, "You can't—there must be something wrong with you," the internal dialogue is terminated prematurely. We say prematurely, because indeed there was enough transparency to recognize that there were two strong emotions towards God that did not seem compatible. But to leave the matter there is to curtail the movement toward intimate friendship with God and others.

A young woman comes to mind who wanted to address the issue of her same-sex attraction. After a few sessions I asked if she had broached the topic with her spiritual director, knowing the central place of spirituality in her life. She replied that she had not brought up the topic. As we explored why she hadn't, she came to see two motives at work in herself. First, she was mad, hurt, and confused. Much of this was directed toward God, the one whom she loves. She had not wished for or chosen her sexual orientation, which was now greatly complicating her life. Second, part of the difficulty lay in that she had no idea of how her orientation was going to fit in with her faith life. Consequently, to bring to her spiritual director the topic of her orientation would require her to be transparent about her conflicted feelings towards God *and* her sexual orientation.

Vulnerability

One cannot be transparent without incurring some measure of vulnerability. This is readily apparent to the people we work with, and it comes up eventually. They understand that there are potential consequences to disclosing oneself to a friend. We simply don't get to control how the other person may respond to our act of transparency, and that makes us vulnerable. We have had more than a few clients/directees state, in effect, that "If you can guarantee me that her response to my disclosure will be positive, I'll do it." And, of course, we can't. The best we can do is be realistic about the likelihood of a positive response from a friend. Can you accept that the desired outcome is not certain? Can your friendship survive a non-supportive response?

BOUNDARIES

With the capacity to be transparent in friendship comes the necessity of maintaining healthy boundaries as well. Many friends have become former friends because of a boundary being transgressed. What is sad and quite common is that in many instances, the offending party was not aware of the mistake. Too often, the person who was offended retreats from the friendship with little or no explanation. What is different about the boundaries in healthy, intimate friendship is that they are discussed as needed and mutually respected.

One source of misunderstanding among friends in regard to boundaries arises from differences in personal disclosure. I may have no trouble sharing about my family of origin. But I may be quite uncomfortable disclosing personal financial information. You may be the opposite. Intimate, healthy friends are able to identify, discuss, and respect boundaries around particular topics.

We also appear to vary in how we define what constitutes an appropriate physical boundary in friendship. A colleague lightheartedly addressed this subject in regard to a region of the United States where he lived for several years. He summed up their stance toward physical intimacy among friends and family by saying, "A handshake goes a long way." "But," I protested, "what if your friend has just had something awful or wonderful happen to him—wouldn't you give him a hug then?" With just the slightest amusement on his face he replied patiently, "A handshake goes a long way."

There does not appear to be a direct connection between how much friends/family hug or kiss and how close they are. It's tempting to assume so, but experience suggests otherwise. Some folks embrace and kiss regularly. For others, a handshake indeed goes a long way. Recognizing and respecting each other's sensibilities in regard to physical affection is a mark of mature friendship.

Healthy boundaries in intimacy support the core values and self-respect of the other. A relationship that erodes our integrity as the cost of maintaining the friendship carries too high a price.

AFFIRMATION

To affirm is to state and demonstrate the truth of one's regard for another. It is a necessary and invaluable generosity present in deep friendship. The affirmations offered at memorial services are always nice to hear. What a wonderful thing for the person being eulogized to have received some of that in life, as well. Sometimes the affirmation we bestow on a friend is specific to a situation. In other instances, the affirmation simply flows from the realization that you are blessed with a great and good friend. We affirm each other with affection, playfulness, words, acts of kindness, and respect.

As Jesus arises from the water newly baptized, we hear these words from the third chapter of Matthew: "This is my Son, the Beloved, with whom I am well pleased" (Matt 3:17). It is the affirmation of the Father. But are we affirmed by the Father, as well? Are you and I his beloved children in whom he is well pleased? Certainly, we don't fare very well in comparison with Jesus. If perfect obedience to the Father's will is necessary to obtain God's affirmation, then only Jesus can have it. We believe, however, that each one of us is affirmed by God by virtue of his decision to create us in his image and to love us always. Parenting provides an analogy. The affirming love of a parent for her two-year-old is not based on that child's perfect obedience. The child is beloved because it is her parent's nature to be pleased with her. God's affirmation of us flows from his character, from his gracious, loving disposition toward us.

Affirmation is not a luxury. A second pair of shoes is a luxury compared to affirmation, which is food for the journey. It sustains us through rough times. Many of us were raised under the prevailing notion that it was best not to compliment a child too much. An overly-praised child might become egotistical, lacking in humility. Many individuals have related to us that affirmation was dispensed in their families in proportions worthy of a radioactive isotope. It is not an exaggeration to say that a great number of adults work very hard to earn the affirmation they did not receive as children.

A man recounted how, from an early age, he had helped his father with the family business. The work was difficult, the hours long, but he spent that time willingly with his father. He asked, "Am I being petty for wondering if it would have been too much for him to have given me a kiss on the forehead once in awhile?" There is something innately healthy in us that claims the right to affection from our parents. Its presence or absence in our childhood sends us down a particular path. To know the affirmation of affection as a child is to sense deeply that you are worth loving and that your love is accepted. Children, in particular, have the unfortunate tendency to trace the fault back to themselves for significant, negative experiences in their families. What many adults have shared with us is that they grew up with the sense that it was some flaw in them that was responsible for their parents' lack of affection or for their parents' divorce. Even when intellectually capable of recognizing that it was not our fault, we still have to contend with the emotional self-doubt.

It is God's will that children grow up with an experiential understanding of how much they are loved by him. Parents are the natural, intended means by which that understanding is to be imparted. When that does not happen for us, we have the spiritual and psychological task of how to live out the relationship he intends between him, ourselves, and others.

ACCOUNTABILITY

Accountability is holding each other to the values we espouse. If our friend is married, we have an obligation to support his marriage. If our friend behaves in a manner detrimental to the well-being of his marriage, we owe him the favor of holding him accountable. If we are unwilling or unable to do so, our role becomes more one of accomplice than friend. For some, unfortunately, friendship carries the implicit understanding that loyalty requires collusion.

Affirmation is what we need and want to hear. We also need accountability, but find it difficult to tolerate. We like affirmation because it is as water to the plant. Accountability feels more like pruning. "Well meant are the wounds a friend inflicts, but profuse are the kisses of an enemy" (Prov 27: 6). Intimate friendship cannot be fully realized without accountability. Without it we avoid the discipline of love that forms us into integrated adults. It is a mature person who will hold her friend accountable and who will accept being held accountable.

A woman in her thirties lived with her parents. She led a sheltered life, by her own account. She came for counseling because she wanted to make some significant changes in her life. She wanted the responsibilities, relationships, and experiences she believed an adult her age should have. After several sessions she asked if she could transfer to another therapist in the community health center. She was told that she could certainly do that. The therapist was curious, however, to know the reason for her request. She said that she didn't mean to hurt his feelings, but she had not made the kind of progress she had hoped for and felt a change of therapist might help. He asked if they could review her case together. They reviewed the incremental changes they agreed to that would indicate that she was progressing in the areas of employment and socializing with peers. They had agreed on goals that were realistic and achievable so that she would be encouraged along the way. She was asked which task she had attempted so far. She replied, "None of them." He asked if she would work harder for another therapist. She paused a bit before answering that she probably would not. They had a good discussion for the rest of the session. She realized that the idea of making changes in her life was attractive, but she was too scared to begin the journey right then. Maybe someday she would be. She was always welcome to come back. He felt an obligation to help her recognize the state of her motivation to change, without shaming her.

Another person related an instance of being held accountable by the Holy Spirit. He had used marijuana for several years. He knew that his habit could not be reconciled with his spirituality. He tried several times to quit on his own. One day he was home alone, thinking about this very issue. He heard a voice within speak firmly and with kindness. The message was that he should choose which road he wanted to be on because he may not have many more chances to do so. He said that he was not sure if the Spirit meant that he might not live much longer to choose or that he was in danger of losing the will to change. Either way, it was quite clear to him that he was at a crossroad with significant consequences for his future. He related that after many years of sobriety he continues to be grateful for God's intervention in his life.

CONCLUSION

We have placed these four skills of intimate friendship in the same chapter because they complement and support each other in practice. To speak of being appropriately transparent is to subsume the existence of boundaries. A person who has boundaries without the practice of transparency has walls that preclude close relationships. Affirmation in friendship without accountability is indulgence. Accountability without affirmation becomes insufferable.

Discussion Questions

1. It seems that significant growth is often accompanied by some measure of discomfort. What discomfort have you experienced during a time of growth?
2. What contradictory feelings have you had about God, a friend, or a family member? What did you do with those feelings?
3. Is it easier for you to be vulnerable to God or to others?
4. How did you respond the last time someone crossed one of your boundaries?
5. In what area of your life are you particularly cautious about sharing information?

6. How are you about affirming your friends?
7. Did you grow up being affirmed at home?
8. How was affection expressed in your family?
9. How do you respond when a friend or family member needs to be held accountable or when you are held accountable?

CHAPTER 7

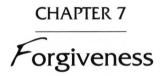

Forgiveness

FORGIVING OTHERS

Forgiveness is a generosity informed by humility and gratitude. Even if we could count all the ways we have been wrong, surely most of us would stop before the end out of despair or exhaustion. It is God's mercy, his forgiveness, that prevents us from being overwhelmed by our failings.

When God speaks of his covenant relationship with his people, forgiveness is often included, as we find in the seventh chapter of 2 Chronicles:

> "If my people who are called by my name humble themselves, pray, seek my face, and turn from their wicked ways, then will I hear from heaven, and will forgive their sin and heal their land." (2 Chr 7:14)

And nearby in the Old Testament we find:

> "But you are a God ready to forgive, gracious and merciful, slow to anger and abounding in steadfast love, and you did not forsake them." (Neh 9:17)

We are lost without forgiveness. In its absence we cannot thrive in our relationship with God, with others, or even with ourselves. Forgiveness allows us to find our way home. It is the counterweight to our imperfections as friends. It is proof that we value relationship above personal grievance. Within the context of friendship, an offense is a sign that there is an issue to be addressed by the parties involved. To be sure, it is an uncomfortable sign—but a sign nonetheless. So many friendships are lost because we take the offense to mean that we cannot be friends. The offense is seen as decisive rather than instructive or corrective.

Forgiveness is so necessary to our well being that God has joined us at the proverbial hip through it. Jesus could not have stated it any more clearly than in Matthew 6:14–15. "For if you forgive others their trespasses, your heavenly Father will also forgive you; but if you do not forgive others, neither will your Father forgive your trespasses."

We cannot receive any more forgiveness than we offer to each other: That is a sobering proposition. We submit, however, that we are allowed and enabled to forgive by God. He gives us the freedom to forgive. Forgiveness is born of God's will that we neither be defined by the wounds we cause nor those we receive.

Forgiveness is a hard lesson from God. Our preference generally is to forgive only when we have run out of viable options. Consequently, forgiveness becomes an extraordinary and exceptional act on our part. But Jesus calls us to forgive others in the same way we receive his forgiveness—regularly and generously. "Then Peter came and said to him, 'Lord, if another member of the church sins against me, how often should I forgive? As many as seven times?' Jesus said to him, 'Not seven times, but, I tell you, seventy-seven times'" (Matt 18:21–22). Peter's question is ours too. We know that forgiveness is necessary, but when is enough, enough? Implied in his response to Peter is the answer: You can cease forgiving when you no longer need my forgiveness.

Yet there are instances in which the offense is so egregious, so profoundly damaging, that forgiveness seems out of the question. Many of us have wondered on occasion if God really thought through this business of forgiveness. There are things that happen to others or us that just seem unforgivable. It is such a personal matter that it would not be my place to tell someone that they have to forgive the person who hurt them. It can be a difficult, complicated process to move from being wounded to being liberated from the effects of the offense. That process should be respected, for it is the Holy Spirit's doing. There is no timetable to go by. There is just God's grace—his love in action—available and willing to take us from victim to survivor to fully engaged in living.

Perhaps the best example of the dynamics of forgiveness in the New Testament is afforded by the Parable of the Prodigal Son in St. Luke's Gospel, chapter 15. There are three main characters in the story: the father, the younger son, and the elder son. The father is an icon into the heart of God, and each of the sons is a mirror image of ourselves in this arena of forgiveness. The father has been described by Pope John Paul II as the definitive picture of God in the New Testament,[1] and one can see why. He simply loves his sons, even his younger son, who has asked for his inheritance and has gone off to have a good time. When the boy's money is spent, he crawls back home confessing that he has sinned against God and against his father. His motives for his return home, however, are somewhat mixed. He is going home because he is hungry and unable to feed himself. Hunger, real "gut" need, powerfully composes his mind, and there is also the beginning of repentance and the need to seek forgiveness. His motives are not pure but mixed, just as ours so often are. The father runs out to greet him, and has obviously been watching and waiting to welcome his son home. There is no recrimination on the father's part, just sheer delight in the return of his son, safe and well, and safe and well in more ways than his son knows.

The welcome home party now takes place. The older brother, returning from work in his father's fields, asks a servant about this feasting, and the servant reports his brother's return. The elder brother is furious and will not enter the party. So, as with the younger brother, his father comes out to him. This father's love makes him take initiatives to ensure the well-being of others. The self-righteous elder son disowns his brother. He speaks of him as "this son of yours," not as "my brother."

Further, this good-living man draws into the story the comment about prostitution (v. 30). There is no direct mention of sexual wrongdoing before the sanctimonious elder brother introduces it. Perhaps there is lust in his heart, a heart he has chosen to harden. He's not as good, as righteous, as he seems. The elder brother, too, is a reflection of us. Especially when it comes to forgiveness, we are so often parsimonious, small-minded, unlike the God/father who is magnanimous. Our thriving is found in allowing God to bring us home to authentic and costly forgiveness.

In practice, forgiveness takes various forms. There is forgiveness that minimizes the severity of the offense. The person may apologize, but it seems almost optional because it is "understood" that it will happen again. We see this in families who want the matter over with without having to contend with the extent of the problem. Someone may have an ongoing addiction or be chronically abusive or irresponsible. His or her behavior is overlooked or minimized by the family.

Another kind of forgiveness does demand a sincere apology with a change in behavior. From that point, however, the response of the offended person may vary. She may decide not to forgive—for the time being or as a finality. She may decide to forgive, but the friendship is modified as a result of the offense. For example, perhaps her friend stole from her. She accepts her apology, but the friend no longer has a key to her home as she once did. There is, as well, forgiveness with full restitution of privileges. This is the forgiveness that God offers us: reconciliation in full.

There is yet another type of forgiveness that is nearly as curious as it is profound. The offending person does not ask for forgiveness. He may deny there is anything for which to apologize. The person who hurt us may no longer even be alive. But we need to rid ourselves of the toxic consequences of the offense, of the power it has over us. Otherwise, it feels like we are being held hostage by the other person's refusal or inability to participate in closure. It is a healing that is finally too necessary to leave undone. So we take the burden to God. We leave it with him. And if it follows us home, we take it back to the cross. It is a journey of faith, a deep recognition that we cannot, that we must not, carry the wound any longer.

This is a mystical exchange we make with God, one that Jesus invites: "Come to me, all you that are weary and carrying heavy burdens, and I will give you rest. Take my yoke upon you, and learn from me; for I am gentle and humble in heart, and you will find rest for your souls. For my yoke is easy, and my burden is light" (Matt 11:28–30). And in this exchange of burdens, what is it that we take upon ourselves? Perhaps it is choosing to be intimately identified with Christ the Forgiver, the one whom the tomb could not hold. It is a claiming of the promise that, as God's children, we do not have to remain entombed by wounds or bitterness. We are granted the liberty to leave the matter finally between God and the offending person. As much as by what we take up, the abundant life in Christ is known by what we are enabled to release.

Perhaps we can get a better sense of the theology of forgiveness and its fruits if we turn to the world of imagination, the world of fiction. In particular, I have in mind the novel of the

Irish writer, Nuala O'Faolain, *My Dream of You.*² Having read O'Faolain's novel, I suspect that it is quite autobiographical, in part revealing something of her own story. The novel is a narrative of threat becoming a gift, of estrangement giving way to forgiveness and reconciliation. The main character is Kathleen De Burca, an Irish woman who is now fifty, unmarried, and has just quit her job as a travel journalist working for a prestigious travel magazine. Although born and brought up in Ireland, Kathleen has lived in London for twenty-eight years. During that time she has never gone back, or we might say that she has never gone home, as an exile might put it.

She hasn't gone home because she is estranged from her family, her country, her religious faith, and from herself. She is estranged from the De Burca family, a dysfunctional family if ever there was one. The father spent almost no time with his children. He was a civil servant working in Dublin, where he would spend the week, coming back at the weekend—I don't say coming home—because he was so remote from the real tortured texture of the De Burca family lives. His wife, Kathleen's mother, is a very depressed woman who seems unable to care for herself or her children. She spends most of the day in bed, doesn't clean, and doesn't cook. She lacks self-esteem, and while her husband and she may have been in love at one time, she seems bound now in a union of loveless sex and complete dependence on her husband.

The mother dies of cancer, and Kathleen does not return for the funeral. She blames her father for not caring for her mother. Her younger brother dies, and she refuses to go back. Her father also dies, but still she does not go home. She just about gives up the practice of her Catholic faith, not so much denying God or the Church as just drifting away from practice. Kathleen sums up her life in these words: "I have never taken an unhurried look at the people by whom I was formed, wanting nothing but to see clearly....My family has been the same size since I ran out of Ireland. Mother? Victim. Nora and me and Danny and poor little Sean? Neglected victims of her victimhood. Villain? Father. Old-style Irish Catholic patriarch; unkind to wife, unloving to children, harsh to young Kathleen when she tried to talk to him."[3]

Kathleen's own life has been quite empty. Successful in terms of her career, she has had a number of lovers, with no relationship lasting very long. She wonders why no man finds her companionable to the point of commitment. Being constantly on the move, traveling the world for her magazine, suits her down to the ground. She loves seeing new, different, and exotic places, and meeting new people. Her best friend is one of her colleagues from work, Jimmy. Whatever she has revealed about herself over the course of her life has been to this man. He knows her deep estrangement from family, home, and faith, and in his own way, now and again, prompts her reconciliation.

Jimmy dies very suddenly of a heart attack. This death brings about slowly and deliberately Kathleen's journey towards reconciliation. She cries out in her pain: "My one and only life slipped past and I never even noticed."[4] She goes back to Ireland, revisits what family she has left, pays her respects in the cemetery, and begins to pray, if only in fits and starts. She learns to forgive and to be forgiven. She continues to make mistakes, but she also begins to reach out to help someone who has just been bereaved, whose mother has died, and in reaching out she minimally begins to find something of her parents, her homeland, her faith, and herself. As she leaves Ireland again at the end of the book after her visit, a real and profound sense of reconciliation-through-forgiveness takes place in her life. Kathleen says: "No one looking at me would guess that I was praying. Let there be a heaven. Let Mammy be in heaven. Let there be something for her because she had such a hard life.…Mammy, please if you still exist, please be somewhere where you are loved, and the cold circle of neglect that was around you in life, please let it be burned away."[5]

If I had to describe Kathleen De Burca in summary fashion, it would be like this: She has been hurt by life, victimized; she has built walls and barriers to keep others out, and she judges those closest to her with an inflexible absoluteness. She is estranged and absolutely unable to forgive. Slowly, the process of forgiveness and reconciliation heals the hollow of her heart.

May God bless us with memory for the forgiveness we have received and for his enduring mercy toward us. Lord, grant us the courage to glorify your name. May we receive from your hands the courage to forgive.

FORGIVING GOD

In the Gospel according to John, chapter 11, we have a poignant story that begins with Jesus letting down his friends. At least it must have seemed so to some who were there. Lazarus was gravely ill, and his sisters sent for Jesus. John emphasizes the depth of their mutual friendship by noting that this Mary was the one who anointed Jesus, wiping his feet with her hair. John also lets us know that Jesus was not very far away. In fact, others came right away when they heard of Lazarus' condition. But not Jesus. He stayed away a few more days. On purpose.

Have you ever experienced, even in your most private moment as a believer, that God didn't come when you needed him? He didn't heal when he could have? He didn't give what was so badly needed, even though for him it would not be much? If God has never disappointed you, great is your faith— may your tribe increase! For the rest us, we know something of Mary and Martha waiting for Jesus—anxious, frustrated, fearful, confused. And what of the others who came, who knew Jesus personally, or at least knew of him? Why won't Jesus come? He has healed complete strangers. Where is he for this family who shares its heart and home with him?

It is important for our present and future relationship with God for us to forgive him. Not, of course, because he has done anything wrong. God is sovereign: He is not accountable to us. The entire book of Job testifies to the sovereignty of Yahweh. The forgiveness we speak of, then, is particular to our condition in relationship to our Creator. It is not forgiveness for being wronged by God; it is forgiveness for the sense of being wronged that we have experienced. It is a reconciliation that acknowledges what we may have tried to place outside of our experience with God.

Many of us have uttered in our hearts our own painfully similar words to those of Martha, "Lord, if you had been here, my brother would not have died" (John 11:21). What do we do with these disappointments? Unattended, they exert a cumulative effect on our faith. We withdraw a bit from God, no longer daring to ask for much in order to avoid further disappointment. We still consider ourselves believers, but our belief is bruised. If this is an issue for you, speak about it with someone you trust with your spirituality. Bring it to the table with God. Pray about it, search the scriptures for perspective, and talk it through until there is peace with God.

FORGIVING OURSELVES

Most people of faith we speak with do believe that they have received God's forgiveness. It is forgiving ourselves that seems to be the real problem. I may ask a client with this difficulty if she can't forgive herself because she is better than others and should suffer more. "No, of course not," she will reply. Well, is she worse than others, is that why she should suffer more? "No," she will say, "I'm not better or worse than others. I'm just the same." So, the answer is not there. We get it intellectually but not emotionally.

What some clients have found helpful is the concept of an internal dialogue between the older, reasonable sibling and the younger one who can't accept forgiveness. The older sibling is kind and firm with the younger sibling when he or she begins the self-recrimination. Visually, it is the older sibling sitting down with the younger one, patiently and firmly explaining that the matter has been forgiven by God. This means that we are going to think, feel, and act like a forgiven person. The talks may be frequent and intense at first because the younger sibling will resist change. Eventually, the protests should diminish in frequency and intensity.

The idea here is that, rather than doing battle with that obsessive, unforgiving part of ourselves, one utilizes firm, loving patience to direct the internal dialogue toward the reality of forgiveness in Christ.

GUILT

It seems appropriate here to speak to the subject of guilt in the context of forgiveness. For the purpose of our discussion, we speak of guilt as the combination of realizing we have done wrong and feeling bad about it—an intellectual and emotional experience of culpability and remorse, a necessary prelude to forgiveness.

There can be too much guilt, but there certainly can be too little. I have interviewed individuals for the legal system who seemed to have little capacity for guilt or empathy. It is quite uncomfortable to realize that this is the case for the person I am sitting alone with in a small room. Their profound deficits become apparent in the course of inquiring about their offenses, how they feel about committing the offenses, and what impact they have had on their victims. I have worked with people burdened with excessive guilt and with those who experience too little. I prefer the former.

In Genesis, chapter 39:9, Joseph endures the sexual harassment of Potiphar's wife. He replies to her insistent advances by stating, "How then could I do this great wickedness, and sin against God?" Whatever she had to offer was more than offset for Joseph by imagining himself breaking faith with his employer and with God.

One of the finest examples of healthy guilt is presented in Psalm 51, known as the *Miserere*. David has committed adultery with Bathsheba. He presents himself before God without excuses, guilty and in need of forgiveness:

> Have mercy on me, O God,
>   according to your steadfast love;
> according to your abundant mercy
>   blot out my transgressions.
> Wash me thoroughly from my iniquity,
>   and cleanse me from my sin. (vv. 1–2)

> Create in me a clean heart, O God,
>   and put a new and right spirit within me. (v. 10)

> The sacrifice acceptable to God is a broken spirit;
>   a broken and contrite heart, O God, you will not
>   despise. (v. 17)

Healthy guilt—that which is given of God—draws us to him and to fellowship. Unhealthy guilt motivates us to hide from God and avoid communion with fellow believers. Note that in Psalm 51 David's full acknowledgment of his wrong is moving him toward the Father. This is life-giving, life-affirming culpability. The central purpose of guilt is to bring us back into relationship. The kind of guilt we practice becomes increasingly unhealthy with each hour it keeps us out of relationship with God, others, and ourselves.

Discussion Questions

1. Has there been a time when you felt defined by an emotional wound? How did you work through it?
2. Is there someone you feel the need to forgive but have not been able to?
3. Is it more difficult for you to forgive or ask for forgiveness?
4. What has been the sticking point when you have had trouble forgiving yourself?
5. Has God disappointed you? How have you dealt with that?
6. How would you characterize the way you usually respond to guilt?

CHAPTER 8

*U*nder a *C*ommon *B*lessing

How does sexuality relate to spirituality other than obviously complicating each other's existence? After all, one of them appears rooted in bodily desire and the other in the desire of the soul. If sexuality and spirituality were people, they couldn't be more different than Esau and Jacob.

The twenty-fifth chapter of Genesis says that Esau and Jacob were twins. In appearance and temperament, however, they could not be more dissimilar. The same applies to sexuality and spirituality. They jostle around inside us as the brothers did in Rebekah's womb. We feel confused, uncomfortable and ask, as did she, "If it is to be this way, why do I live?" (v. 22). Let us carry three ideas along with us as we enter into this discussion of sexuality and spirituality. First, Esau and Jacob had a common source. They were children of the same parents. Second, these siblings had their well-documented troubles along the way. Third, after a lengthy estrangement they were reconciled—they accepted each other.

COMMON GROUND

Given of God

Sexuality and spirituality do have the same Father. Yet, spirituality is the child we love to talk about; sexuality is the troublesome offspring—the black sheep—of whom we would rather not be asked. But God is comfortable with the topic from the very beginning. In the creation story, God said it is not good for man to be the only creature in the garden who is alone. Eve and Adam make paradise complete for each other. God tells them to be fruitful and multiply, which is a poetic way of saying, "Make love; give me some grandchildren, already!" It is all stated rather matter-of-factly. The naturalness of their sexual relationship corresponds to the naturalness of their relationship with the Father. "And the man and his wife were both naked, and were not ashamed" (Gen 2:25). God made sexuality. It is good because God is good.

Sexual Attraction

Sexuality is our attraction to another person in a way that is categorically distinct from the way we experience platonic friendship or familial love. We see this romantic attraction at work in us from an early age. I was walking through the preschool area of a church on the way to a meeting. A group of children were with their teacher in the hallway. I heard the teacher speak to one of the boys: "If you like her, Jeremy, just say so—don't pull her hair." I had to smile because I was that boy once upon a time. Romantic attraction is the basis of normal sexuality. To speak of one's sexual orientation is to identify one's attraction to females or males.

A client asked if we could discuss his sexuality. I inquired about his sexual orientation. Without hesitation he answered that his orientation was heterosexual. And to what was he physically attracted in women? "What do you mean," he asked. Now it was my turn to be puzzled. "I mean…are you attracted to a woman's hair, her smile, her eyes, her mouth? Do you tend to notice her breasts, her buttocks, her legs, or some combination of attributes?" I thought I had given him plenty of options at that point. "Well," he replied, "I'm not really aroused that way by women." I answered that perhaps his orientation was not heterosexual after all, because to be sexually oriented is to experience attraction. No attraction, no orientation.

At our next session he wanted to revisit the topic of his orientation. "You know, I've been thinking, and I do have something that attracts me." He said, "It might seem silly to you, but I like the way the sunlight falls on a woman's neck and highlights the fine little hair on her neck and earlobes. I think that's sexy." He seemed a bit sheepish but relieved to have said it. What seemed important was for him to recognize attraction as integral to normal sexuality.

Spiritual Attraction

Attraction and desire are no less central to our spirituality, to our relationship with God, than they are to our sexuality. He desires us. He loves us with all his being. The Church is depicted in scripture as the Bride of Christ, the focus of God's desire. And that same Church, to be sure, is nothing less than you and me. It is an intimate, passionate relationship that is offered to us as redemptive throughout the Bible. We can hear God's desire for us in the call and response of the lover and the beloved in Song of Songs. Jesus, in the twelfth chapter of John, declares, "And I, when I am lifted up from the earth, will draw all people to myself" (v. 32). In Christ's outpouring of himself (*kenosis*) on the cross we, the beloved, grasp something of the depth of his passion for us. What we can offer in response to God's passion for us is our passion for him.

More than anything else, we need an integrated relationship with God, a holistic spirituality. Many of us suffer from a two-tiered spiritual approach. One tier is the sacred; the other is the definitely inferior secular tier. If God has put something of himself into creation, into our sexuality, as we saw in the previous passage from Genesis, then the two-tiered approach not only does not work but cannot work. We are drawn into relationship with our God through the whole of who we are, no exclusions.

RECONCILIATION

Intimacy

Intimacy is the basis for authentic human sexuality. Without intimacy, sexuality is developmentally stalled at the level of self-gratification. It is heat without light. Intimacy is the basis for authentic spirituality as well. Without deep friendship, our encounter with God is, at best, cerebral. It is offering to God an intellectual assent without the embrace of one's deepest self.

Reconciliation, a thriving coexistence of sexuality and spirituality, is also made possible by the practice of intimacy between them. We speak to some of the practical aspects of that intimacy in the following sections.

Forgiveness

On a good day we see some sign of growth, of maturity, in how we live our faith or in how we express our sexuality. But it is rare for most of us to experience our spirituality and sexuality in a dialogue that is fundamentally hopeful. Instead, what many of us bear witness to is an estrangement between our spirituality and sexuality.

Our sexuality has been demonized, marginalized, and given a second-class status relative to our spirituality. Our spirituality doesn't know what to do with sexuality. Out of frustration it seems to say, "Just go sit in the corner and try not to embarrass me for once!" Or "We'll talk about this later." But we never seem to get around to having that talk. And our sexuality has not learned how to take spirituality into account in its expression. Consequently, there are those regrettable occasions during which we behave sexually without regard to our relationship with God. Our sexuality can also be dismissive toward our spirituality, as if to say, "That's fine for you to live in your world of spiritual ideals, but I have to contend with this body and its desires." The accumulation of bruised interactions between our sexuality and spirituality causes them to give up on each other. Our spirituality and sexuality have great need of that God-gift, of that grace that is forgiveness. For it is forgiveness that clears the way to commitment.

Commitment

Commitment between spirituality and sexuality begins with the resolve to keep them in relationship, engaged in dialogue. This requires vigilance and patience, since they are accustomed to acting independently of each other. It will take time for them to adjust to the other's presence. The premise we are operating from is that our sexuality was and is intended as a natural companion to our relationship with God. Attraction to God is meant to inform our attraction to each other. We commit our sexuality and spirituality to each other from the conviction that their reconciliation is of vital importance to our well-being. We have tried managing them separately—and we know that to be ineffective most days and disastrous on occasion. We come, then, to the conclusion that we must learn how to have them relate to each other. This is our commitment.

We know that commitment is taking root between our sexuality and spirituality in the flourishing of a robust relationship. They take hold of each other in friendship. The relationship supersedes particular grievances. There is a lived-out resolve to sustain the friendship in the face of their inability to give themselves to it perfectly. This robustness is an act of faith that comprehends that it is only through intimate friendship that our spirituality and sexuality will ever come to understand the God-intended place each is to have in the life of the other.

Transparency

We have stated that being confused about our response to a situation and sorting through that experience can be useful in the movement toward transparency. Let us look at an example of how our spirituality and sexuality can be transparent to each other. A number of people we have worked with over the years report a similar, distressing event. They are praying, meditating, or worshipping alone or with others. In that moment, unwanted sexual thoughts, images, fantasies come into awareness. The tone in which they report this event ranges from annoyed to scandalized. "What kind of disordered person must I be to have such thoughts in the middle of my communion with God?" This is the very sort of thing that causes one to doubt that spirituality and sexuality can coexist. But let's take a moment to consider another possible explanation for this experience.

Since attraction and desire are basic to both our sexuality and spirituality, is it possible that the stirring of one may, on occasion, elicit the other in the way that a fragrance will sometimes elicit a memory? This dynamic of mutual arousal has been related to us by a number of people of faith. It may be that, when we are interrupted in devotion by sexual thoughts, there is something more benign happening than we feared. What, then, can we do when this occurs?

Imagine yourself sitting on the bank of a stream on a beautiful day. In the periphery of your vision you notice a branch floating in the water. You see it float directly in front of you and pass on downstream. You continue to enjoy the day. Instead of being annoyed, upset, or ashamed of the sexual thoughts, feelings, images that appear during devotion, simply acknowledge their presence and allow them to float on by without engaging them. Return to your communion with God. We have seen encouraging results with this approach. The transparency here is acknowledging and accepting that sexual thoughts and feelings sometimes occur at inconvenient times.

Many years ago my wife's family had the wedding of a relative in their home. In the midst of the wedding vows the family dog, an old, asthmatic, Japanese Spaniel named "Baby" came into the living room wheezing and snorting rather loudly. There was an exchange of incredulous looks and silence for a moment, then quite a bit of laughter over the incongruity of it all. Sometimes our sexuality comes wandering in like that at the most inopportune time. It's not mortal, and we're not under any obligation to act on thoughts or images. So it may be best to let them be on their way and go on with what we're doing. It is perhaps needlessly punitive to assume the worst about ourselves when uninvited thoughts occur.

Boundaries and Accountability

We believe that the full expression of sexuality or spirituality requires the presence of the other. Healthy sexuality is animated by our intimacy with God. He loved us first and best. His is an everlasting love. Our love for each other is sacramental to the extent that it is informed by, and a part of, our relationship with him. A relationship with God that denies our sexuality or our attraction to other adults cannot be complete. In fact, such a stance puts others and us at risk. There are tragic examples readily available of those who separated their sexuality from their spirituality.

It appears that life would be greatly simplified if God would just release us from sexual attraction. Perhaps one time or another that has been the prayer of many of us. In a way it's a prayer for him to make our lives less complicated. Contending with our sexuality forces us to depend on God in a particular way, to seek his presence, to be assured that we are still accepted. As one person said, "Without sexual attraction, I could manage my faith life fairly well on my own." But God gives us this attraction that energizes our relationship with him and with each other. Sexual attraction is here to stay, and it is our task to keep it in an ongoing dialogue with God.

That dialogue is particularly necessary in the presence of strong, mutual attraction to someone without the freedom to enter into that relationship. This is the tension between attraction and faithfulness. It is here that sexuality is accountable to our spirituality, our relationship with God. We are well acquainted with the results of sexual behavior that acts in isolation from our spirituality. We objectify the other. We torment ourselves, obsessing over someone who is not ours to be with. At worst, we become involved with someone at the cost of betraying others and our own core values.

It is not the initial attraction that is the problem. It becomes a problem when we do not contend with that attraction within our yes to God. We know all too well that attraction will guide us on occasion unerringly onto the rocks. Our yes to God is a daily, life-long endeavor of love. It is our passion for God, made possible by God. It is a mature love that shapes our sexuality. It allows us to state with Paul: "It is my eager expectation and hope that I will not be put to shame in any way, but that by my speaking with all boldness, Christ will be exalted now as always in my body, whether by life or by death" (Phil 1:20).

Affirmation

> Not that I have already obtained this, or have already reached the goal; but I press on to make it my own, because Christ Jesus has made me his own. Beloved, I do not consider that I have made it my own; but this one thing I do: forgetting what lies behind and straining forward to what lies ahead, I press on toward the goal for the prize of the heavenly call of God in Christ Jesus. (Phil 3:12–14)

The scriptural account of Esau and Jacob has threads that run the course of their relationship: competition, taking hold, and blessing. These threads weave together at particular moments, becoming something they could not be individually. Esau and Jacob jostled in the womb. Jacob grasps the heel of Esau at their delivery into the world. At his imminent passing, their father, Isaac, takes hold of Esau to give him his rightful blessing as the first born…but he takes hold of Jacob instead. Jacob receives the blessing by deceit. Jacob flees so that his brother will not take hold of him in revenge. Many years later Jacob takes hold of God by the river. He receives a blessing from God through perseverance. With that blessing Jacob moves toward the encounter with his estranged brother, the one he had wronged. Jacob sends gifts ahead of himself, but he must know that if Esau desires retribution, nothing will quench that thirst but his blood. Jacob places himself and his family completely at the mercy of Esau. What we witness at their encounter is a depth of forgiveness, relief, and acceptance that brings to mind the return of the prodigal son. "But Esau ran to meet him, and embraced him, and fell on his neck and kissed him, and they wept" (Gen 33:4). The first blessing Jacob received by deceit, the second through perseverance. He receives this final blessing from his older brother through vulnerability, by submitting his heart in a plea to be reconciled.

Through this epic journey toward each other after so many years of being apart, the brothers at last come to know that they should be together. So it is with sexuality and spirituality: they belong together. They have the same Father. They are under a common blessing.

A man shared an e-mail response he received from a friend who is a pastor. He was trying to find a way to make peace between his spirituality and his sexuality. He shared this challenge with his friend whose response is paraphrased here:

He told him to bring his sexuality to the supper table. He said that Jesus is there ready to break bread with him—and us. It is there that Jesus can bless your sexuality, when it is invited to take its rightful place in your life.

It is no mere coincidence that the common name for the Lord's supper is Eucharist, which means thank you in Greek. Thank you for making us spiritual, capable of relationship with you, and thank you for making us sexual, capable of intimacy with others—and through it all, literally, more integral with you. Amen.

Discussion Questions

1. Is your sexuality part of your relationship with God?
2. Do you remember when sexuality and spirituality became a problem for each other in your life?
3. What influences the particular ways we are attracted to another?
4. Does society teach us whom to be attracted to or is that something that comes from within?
5. What do you think of the idea that attraction is central to our spirituality and sexuality?
6. What difference would it make in your life if your spirituality and sexuality became good friends?

CHAPTER 9

ℛeflections

It was several years ago while I was browsing a secondhand shop in Mount Angel, Oregon, that I saw a piece that was quite different from the other items. It was a small tapestry. It measured about twelve inches across and no more than eighteen inches in length. The patterns and bright colors brought to mind Latin America. It was two thirds of the way finished, with the remainder of the red threads moving up to the top where the two wooden sticks of the rustic loom awaited. It hangs in my office now.

In a way my life seems to resemble it. The remaining threads are there, but what will the rest of the pattern look like? Am I waiting on God to show me? Maybe God is waiting on me, to hear me say, "Yes Father," with all of myself. Or perhaps the loom is already moving and will continue to move throughout eternity. It is solace to believe that there is not a deadline for becoming like Jesus. This gives me hope that the embrace of spirituality, intimacy, and sexuality in my life has begun and will continue—by his grace. And I suspect that our small, individual tapestries are destined to be united in witness to the Weaver.

I used to visit a dear, strong, devout lady named Margaret at the retirement home where she lived. I imagined that my visits were ministry of a sort, and so they were. She ministered to *me* generously. After a number of visits together, she shared a story from her youth. She was a nursing student and met a young man. They became quite fond of each other and talked of getting married. He was in business, an ambitious fellow. After several months he had the bittersweet news for Margaret that he had been promoted—a promotion that required a transfer several states away. She was sad for herself but happy for him. She had to stay and finish her course of studies and training. He promised to write and call regularly, which he did for some months. Eventually, though, the calls stopped and the letters became infrequent. One day she received a call from him that he was back in town on business, and he wanted her to come downtown to his hotel so he could see her. There was a trolley to downtown that ran near the nurses' dormitory, a trolley that didn't go nearly fast enough for her that day.

They sat down together. She was eager to say and hear him say all the things that meant they were still a couple. He said that he needed to see her because he felt he owed it to her to tell her personally that he was dating someone else. That is why he stopped calling, and he couldn't bring himself to tell her by letter. She took the trolley downtown but walked the few miles back home that day. Margaret said it was the most painful time of her young life.

Many years later she received a call from the same fellow. Once again he said that he was in town and would like to have breakfast with her. She composed herself and said that she and her husband would be glad to see him. The three of them spoke of small, safe things over breakfast. Finally, the former boyfriend said to Margaret, "Many years ago I had the chance to marry you, and I want to tell you that it was the biggest mistake of my life not to. My life was miserable with the person I left you for. I was the fool, Margaret."

To her husband, he said, "You are very lucky to be her husband." The husband replied, "I know." Her story brought a few tears to both of us. "So," I asked, "people sometimes abandon us but God never does?" A slight nod and smile was her answer.

Another lesson Margaret taught me had to do with a fellow resident where she lived. He was a pastor for decades. Margaret knew him many more years than I. Now, advanced in dementia, he walked about the facility greeting one and all. I remarked to Margaret that I remembered him as being so dignified. She made sure our eyes met before she responded, "He still is."

Now, several years after her death, her two lessons speak to our topic. In desiring and working to integrate spirituality, intimacy, and sexuality in our lives, we refuse to abandon them. We claim them in God's name. We respond to the challenge of it with a faithfulness of God's making. It is God's faithfulness that dignifies us. He is the Lover, we are the beloved. Our dignity is rooted in redemptive relationship.

THE FIRST VOCATION

In our part of the world the word "vocation" is frequently heard in reference to one's commitment to religious or clerical life. Vocation is also used to describe the commitment to marriage. We propose, however, that the first vocation is the commitment to becoming a whole, healthy human being. All other vocations are made possible by the first. Intimate friendship is the foundation for authentic spirituality and sexuality. It is the genuine response of the beloved to the lover—to God our Creator, to friends and family, and to our romantic partner. It is the profound love of intimate friendship, graced by God, that animates us with the courage to take the initiative to ensure the well-being of those we love. We find the courage to risk setting aside our self-image, defenses, addictions, and insecurities for a simpler life, a life embraced by the Father and capable of embracing others. It is a simpler life because God makes possible the removal of the clutter between him and us.

It is a simpler life but not a simple one because of attraction. Attraction draws us to God and to each other—it animates us. But it also evokes our propensity to possess, to control, to objectify the other. Attraction can find its way to genuinely intimate relationship or to self-gratification. Among people of faith, some wish to expunge attraction to others in service of being attracted exclusively to God. This repression or suppression of attraction, however, comes with its own set of potential consequences.

If we contend with our attractions intentionally, we have a much better chance of influencing the outcome. We have listened to people describe with astonishment an incident of sexual acting out on their part that they did not see coming. Their efforts to put their sexuality out of awareness only served to place them at risk.

The full, life-affirming expression of spirituality and sexuality requires that each be present to the other. A spirituality that brackets sexuality to the side is weakened by its exclusion, compromised by an important facet of oneself left unblessed, unloved. Sexuality, enacted independently of one's relationship with God, orients itself toward self-gratification and loses the deeper joy of fulfillment.

Spirituality and sexuality are reconciled, then, by the practice of intimacy between them. We have spoken to some of the constituent skills of intimacy in the hope that something of value can be gleaned. We acknowledge both the necessity and difficulty of living a life with intimate friendship as the foundation for our spirituality and sexuality. As mentioned previously, there are moments of spiritual lucidity in which we allow ourselves to live in God's embrace, and we wish those moments would become hours and days and a way of living all the time. We see God calling the people we work with to this life. We experience that same call. We have written this book not because we have succeeded in living this way, but because we desire its fruition in our lives as well.

Its fruition is our birthright; it is ours to claim and commit to with all of ourselves. We are under a common blessing, a blessing bestowed by no common god but by our God, the source of all creation. Those he blesses cannot be unblessed, those he loves cannot be unloved. Only let us take hold of the One who loved us first, who loves us best.

Discussion Questions

1. What part of you feels unfinished?
2. What patterns have you discerned in yourself?
3. What clutter is there between you and God?
4. What clutter is there between you and a friend or family member?
5. What would be the first sign to you—in the way you think, feel, or act—that your spirituality and sexuality are becoming friends?
6. In what ways would it change your life to live in God's embrace?

*N*otes

CHAPTER ONE

1. Gerard M. Hopkins, "Thee, God," in *Gerard Manley Hopkins: Poems and Prose*, selected and with an introduction and notes by W. H. Gardener (New York and London: Penguin Books, 1985), 83. Emphasis added.

CHAPTER FOUR

1. Denis Ngien, "Richard of St. Victor's Condilectus," *European Journal of Theology* 12 (2003): 77–92.

CHAPTER FIVE

1. Michael Purcell, *Mystery and Method: The Other in Rahner and Levinas* (Milwaukee: Marquette University Press, 1998), 172.

2. William Barclay, *The Daily Bible Study Series*, vol. 1, The Gospel of John, rev. ed. (Philadelphia: The Westminster Press, 1975), 217.

CHAPTER SEVEN

1. Pope John Paul II, *Dives in misericordia* 1Y.5, 1980.

2. Nuala O'Faolain, *My Dream of You* (New York: Penguin Group USA, RiverHead Books, 2001).

3. Ibid., 21.

4. Ibid., 23.

5. Ibid., 526.

Bibliography

Barclay, William. *The Daily Bible Study Series*. Vol. 1, The Gospel of John, rev. ed. Philadelphia: The Westminster Press, 1975.

Hopkins, Gerard M. "Thee, God." In *Gerard Manley Hopkins: Poems and Prose*, selected and with an introduction and notes by W.H. Gardener, 83. New York and London: Penguin Books, 1985.

Ngien, Denis. "Richard of St. Victor's Condilectus." *European Journal of Theology* 12 (2003): 77–92.

O'Faolain, Nuala. *My Dream of You*. New York: Penguin Group USA, RiverHead Books, 2001.

Pope John Paul II. *Dives in misericordia,* 1980.

Purcell, Michael. *Mystery and Method: The Other in Rahner and Levinas*. Milwaukee: Marquette University Press, 1998.